W9-DJG-771

Virtual Combat

A Guide to Distributed Interactive Simulation

David L. Neyland

STACKPOLE
BOOKS

Published by
STACKPOLE BOOKS
5067 Ritter Rd.
Mechanicsburg, PA 17055

This book is not an official publication of the Department of Defense, nor does its publication in any way imply its endorsement by this agency.

Printed in the United States of America

First Edition

10 9 8 7 6 5 4 3 2 1

Cover design by Caroline Stover
Cover art by David L. Neyland

The artwork is the creation of the author using an Apple Power Macintosh 7100/66 AV, KPT Bryce, Strata Studio Pro Blitz, Adobe Photoshop, and Microsoft Powerpoint.

Library of Congress Cataloging-in-Publication Data

Neyland, David L.
    Virtual combat : a guide to distributed interactive simulation / David L. Neyland. — 1st ed.
      p.   cm.
    Includes index.
    ISBN 0-8117-3125-1
    1. Military art and science—Computer simulation. 2. Digital computer simulation. 3. Interactive computer systems.
    UG478.N48   1997
    355'.001'13436—dc21   97–24180
                                      CIP

Special thanks to Sue for supporting me in this endeavor,
to Zack and Thomas for giving up their time on the Mac,
and to Winnie and Pooh for keeping my feet warm
during the long, cold winter.

Contents

Figures

Tables

Introduction

On February 26, 1991, at 1,000 meters east of 72 Easting in the middle of the Iraqi desert, three companies of U.S. M1A1 Abrams battle tanks and M3 Bradley fighting vehicles came across a numerically superior force of 130 Iraqi 12th Armored Division T-72 tanks, armored fighting vehicles, and trucks. In a fierce battle lasting two hours, all the Iraqi forces were destroyed or succumbed to the tactics and operations of the U.S. forces. The battle became known as the Battle of 73 Easting. It is regarded as a critical moment in the campaign to crush the three Iraqi Republican Guard Divisions—the Tawakalna, the Medina, and the Hammurabi—and was a decisive victory for the coalition forces of Desert Storm. One of the crucial factors in the success of the U.S. troops, from their testimonials,[1] was their feeling that they had fought the battle before. Their familiarity with the dynamics of the engagement gave them a significant tactical advantage—it gave them battlespace dominance.

Since February 1991, the Battle of 73 Easting has been refought hundreds of times. Each time, the fight to the death quickens the pulses of the warriors, the smoke and flames obscure their vision, the thrum of the tank engines vibrates in their bones, and the frantic, crackling radio calls make their palms sweat. These instances of déjà vu are no nightmares for the war-weary veterans, for each visit is conducted in a simulation of the real environment. Yet on each and every revisit to the Iraqi desert, new vantage points are observed and new lessons are learned. The time travel back to the desert is deliberate and premeditated. It is made possible through advances in simulation technologies known as Distributed Interactive Simulation.

In December 1993, two years after the Battle of 73 Easting, U.S. forces returned to Southwest Asia to fight again in the sand. This time the Iraqis had crossed the border into Saudi Arabia, and the United States, with no pre-deployment opportunity, had to mass air, sea, and land forces to repel the incursion. The Navy used its new Faststrike missiles to counter incoming SCUDs, the Air Force flew autonomous search-and-strike unmanned air vehicles to find SCUD launchers, and the Army launched its ATACM missiles against the SCUD sites. Army, Navy, and Air Force warfighters sat, stood, and fought side by side, controlling and conducting operations shoulder to shoulder. A new era of joint interaction was born. Joint command and control of the entire battlespace were central to success in these operations, which were known as Zen Regard. But was Zen Regard real? Or did it happen only in the world of Distributed Interactive Simulation?

1

The reliving of the Battle of 73 Easting and the Zen Regard battles in 1993 are two examples of a burgeoning realm of simulation called Distributed Interactive Simulation—more commonly known as DIS. The Battle of 73 Easting occurred in real life and then was immediately recorded for history, to be relived in simulation for training purposes. Zen Regard was a system engineering simulation of a possible future, to be explored ad infinitum to understand the ramifications of future warfighting challenges. Both of these examples are made possible by advances in computer hardware, computer software, computer networking, and computer graphics technology. They represent two principal applications of DIS—training and system engineering.

DISTRIBUTED INTERACTIVE SIMULATION

Electronically hooking together tank, airplane, ship, and other simulators at a variety of locations, and letting warrior-operators in simulators see one another and shoot and be shot at, all in recreations of the real world—this is DIS. Technically speaking, DIS uses high-speed data networks to connect simulators around the world and let their computers interact and "play." DIS creates an artificial world with sufficient realism to allow military personnel to learn, practice, and refine their warfighting skills in an environment with much of the look and feel of an actual battle.

Distributed Interactive Simulation first came to prominence in the Defense community through the sponsorship of General Gordon R. Sullivan, Chief of Staff of the Army. In 1991 he saw the value of recreating the Battle of 73 Easting for training and the utility of recording it for history. Under his purview, the battle was cataloged using the precursor to DIS—SIMNET technology. After the battle and Desert Storm were over, on-site inspection teams were sent to the Iraqi desert to record the action. The historians made detailed records of every twist and turn and gunshot of every participant in the battle, making notes of tank track marks, spent shell casings, and ravaged enemy vehicles. From their exquisitely accurate details, a three-dimensional replay of the battle was programmed into simulation computers so that it could be observed through electronic visualization from any vantage point—in the three dimensions of space and through the fourth dimension of time. Although not interactive in the sense of altering the events and actions of the battle, the recreation of the Battle of 73 Easting was a revolutionary approach to creating a "living history."[2] It was the first simulation to popularize distributed simulation, and is perhaps the most widely viewed and recognized defense simulation to date. It was virtual combat.

As a result of that singular simulation event, significant attention has been focused within the Department of Defense on the applicability and uses of DIS. Although the usefulness of DIS for training has been repeatedly substantiated, the more difficult challenge of applying it as an analytical tool has been addressed merely as a potential virtue worth pursuing. No scientific process was defined to integrate the extrapolations possible in an imaginary world to the machinations of real-world warfare. Perhaps the doorway of training simulation offers an entrée to applying rigor to DIS for system engineering—in the end, specifying simulation engineering for warfighting.

SUPPORT FOR DIS

In spring of 1992, the simulation for the recreation of the Battle of 73 Easting was taken to Congress. A simulation center, replete with helicopter and aircraft simulators and a "flying carpet" out-the-window display, was set up in a Senate conference room for the Senate Conference on Modeling and Simulation. It was connected to a computer network of simulation sites around the world. For nearly an hour, the Department of Defense conducted spontaneous, unscripted warfighting operations, even putting Senate members behind the controls of the simulators. The senators were heartily impressed. It was a heyday in marshaling support for DIS.

Leading the simulation charge up Capitol Hill were Dr. Victor Reis, Director of Defense Research and Engineering, and General Paul Gorman, U.S. Army, (Ret.), Chairman of the 1992 Department of Defense Simulation Policy Study. In his opening statement to the Senate hearings, Dr. Reis said, "Network simulation is a technology that elevates and strengthens the collective problem solving abilities of human beings, people acting as teams, learning and getting better, and it is true whether they are design teams, education teams, training teams, to warfighting teams."[3] General Gorman testified that "all tactical training short of combat itself is a simulation."[4] He added that simulators are a catalyst for comprehension, and that simulation is fundamental to combat readiness for war.[5] A year after the Senate Armed Services Committee hearings, the 1993 report of the Defense Science Board Task Force on Simulation, Readiness, and Prototyping went a step farther in extolling the all-encompassing relevance of simulation by reiterating General Gorman's point that "everything is simulation except combat."[6] The Defense Science Board further reasoned that if we were not actually fighting a war but merely simulating one, the most useful and best simulation available was DIS.

WHY DIS?

How does using DIS contribute to the execution of warfare? Can it help us come to terms with the increasing operational tempo that has become the norm? If simulation is fundamental to combat readiness and is a catalyst for comprehension—but is limited by our ability to verify and validate its alacrity—what role should it play? Does this enthusiasm for simulation merit the ambitious plans we have set in place for it? Can the use of DIS to explore issues in command and control, training, weapon application, combat identification, and joint doctrine development be considered a new type of engineering—simulation engineering for warfighting?

Before attempting to formulate answers to these questions, we must also consider some of the issues facing the use of military forces. Repeatedly throughout the 1990s we have had U.S. forces in combat, on support and relief missions, in operations in places around the globe—in Desert Storm, Bosnia, Somalia, Rwanda, Cuba, Panama, Haiti, and back again. Each event has demonstrated the tremendous strength of the United States as the single remaining global military superpower. Our military technological revolution during the 1970s and 1980s unquestionably augmented our current ability to succeed in these operations. New technologies clearly bolstered our firepower's lethality and precision. But perhaps more surprising was our newfound success directly attributable to the command of information, where we reign supreme in comparison to other military forces.

It is in the realm of "information" that DIS can help shape the future operations of U.S. forces. In an era in which we have technological and information supremacy, we continue to experience marginal success in attacking certain types of targets while protecting our own forces from friendly fire. Both of these problems can be tied directly to our soldiers' lack of the right information at the right place and at the right time. Despite the enormous quantities of data available to us, unless we can acquire and assimilate that one critical data element we need, when we need it, where we need it, and how we need it, we will remain information insolvent. We must find ways to manage our information flow in order to overcome our remaining warfighting deficiencies. We need to learn and understand how to harness the massive influx of information to which we have given birth. We need information dominance. The effectiveness and safety of our forces demand that we find new tools to accomplish this goal. One such tool is DIS—the networking of many types of physically separate simulators—to provide us with a means for learning to cope with the variety, scope, and pace of the blossoming information spectrum. Just as was done in the recreation of the Battle of 73 Easting and Zen Regard, we can use DIS to create an illusion, an experimental battlespace in which to train, to fly, and to fight. DIS will let us learn how to dominate the information of the battlespace, and through it, we can achieve virtual dominance.

DIS can provide us with tools to understand the warfighting environment of the late 1990s—perhaps even letting us practice our warfighting skills under the intense public oversight we have come to expect. The 1990s have emerged as an era burdened by expectations of bloodless war. We are hamstrung by the "CNN phenomenon," whereby real-time public scrutiny decries all civilian enemy casualties, casualties of U.S. forces, or collateral damage to civilian targets. This phenomenon has driven our conduct of war to diverge from Clausewitzian principles. Clausewitz argued for imposing our will on the enemy by applying maximum available force to render the enemy powerless.[7] He believed that distress at the brutality of war was inappropriate to its very nature and that such considerations could not be allowed to inhibit the means of warfighting.

Today, however, the application of force must take into consideration public sentiment. DIS presents an avenue for us to practice and evaluate the means and effects of warfighting. The very nature of DIS—an interactive, recordable battlespace—gives us the opportunity to replay and evaluate our warfighting techniques from a military vantage, as well as from the viewpoint of the scrutinizing public.

So why DIS? Does it contribute to the execution of warfare? How do we apply it as a catalyst for comprehension? What constitutes simulation engineering for warfighting? Bear these questions in mind as we look to the tactical necessities and the issues and roles for DIS.

TACTICAL NECESSITIES
Consider the paramount issue for warfighting: although the methodology of combat may be changing, the tactical necessities have not changed. At the onset of any modern war, timely destruction of certain classes of targets, such as mobile command posts, command and control elements, and mobile antiaircraft and other missiles, is pivotal in preventing the enemy from effectively managing and employing its warfighting forces. Elimination of these classes of targets enables us to wage war more effectively and with a more efficient allocation of our weapon systems against the enemy forces, while simultaneously preventing attack on friendly military and civilian personnel. Our superiority in firepower and precision has enabled us to maintain a successful operational tempo throughout the 1990s that is unparalleled. DIS provides a stage for training that will enable us to amplify that operational tempo. But how do we sensibly extend our training successes with DIS to experiment with new warfighting technologies and operational concepts from an analytical perspective?

The issues of concern to U.S. forces go on and on. The ongoing saga in Bosnia, peacekeeping in Haiti, and monitoring no-fly zones in Southwest Asia are examples of the type of operations in which U.S. forces continue to be involved. Our integrated joint warfighting systems embody capabilities spanning peacetime, crisis, hostilities, and postwarfare. Our forces routinely become geographically intertwined with enemy combatants and civilian noncombatants. But U.S. military operations are expected to apply precise and overwhelming firepower from the ground, the sea, or the air against dispersed hostile forces in an indistinct, amorphous battlespace. And throughout, we expect our joint warfighters to retain cognizance of the participation and vulnerability of all the individual members of the U.S. forces—driving us toward some form of active combat identification. These dichotomies will continue to challenge our ability to manage warfare.

Today, even our overwhelming technological superiority as the world's only military superpower belies our adequacy to counter certain targets and protect our forces and assets. The great SCUD hunt of Desert Storm graphically demonstrated the U.S. shortfall in locating and destroying small forces of elusive mobile missiles. The difficulties encountered raised the specter of information management—collecting and disseminating the right information to the right user at the right time—clearly indicating areas that need improved capability. In June 1995, Dr. John M. Deutch, Director of Central Intelligence, described it this way:

> The effectiveness of U.S. military forces is critically dependent on military commanders having this dominant battlefield awareness . . . that imagery, signals, and human intelligence must be integrated and distributed in a timely fashion to battlefield commanders . . . to give joint force commanders real-time or near-real-time, all-weather, comprehensive, continuous surveillance and information about the battlespace in which they operate.[8]

The importance of situational awareness and operational span of control in the battlespace cannot be more poignantly advanced than by the repeated cases of U.S. and allied ground force casualties due to friendly fire during Desert Storm in 1991 and the subsequent shooting down of U.S. helicopters in Iraq in 1994. Once again we learned that *waging war is an expensive way to discover operational shortfalls or test new warfighting concepts.* A better means would be to experiment within the boundless battlespace of a DIS synthetic world, a place where we can introduce new weapons and concepts at minimal expense and no physical risk. This is a fundamental role for DIS. It draws on the nature of DIS as an interactive, recordable battlespace—giving us the opportunity to replay and evaluate our warfighting techniques from the military vantage. In the process, we will learn new techniques to maintain and utilize our information dominance.

DIS FOR ACTIONABLE COMMAND AND CONTROL

Desert Storm saw an unprecedented allocation of weapons systems to counter the enemy. Now, however, the unconstrained application of overwhelming force runs contrary to our evolving political objectives. We cannot act without regard to ancillary effects, including the effect of negative publicity. Our warfighters must strive to obtain maximum effect with minimum violence. To do this requires information dominance. It levies on us a requirement to synthesize every microdetail of warfare into an executable whole. At the same time, we must retain responsibility for considering the location, action, and interaction of every participant and nonparticipant in the battlespace—every soldier, sailor, aircrew member, and civilian.

Maintaining visibility at the individual combatant level—soldier, sailor, or aircrew—has created a tremendous burden related to management of the information flow. What we should do, when, and with which information should be considered actionable command and control. It translates to those information-based activities that can and must be acted on by human beings, whether by intervention or through active decision making. Using DIS as a tool of exploration, we have a reasonable chance of identifying and addressing issues of actionable command and control. This is the single greatest attribute of DIS and represents the hidden benefit that we unconsciously applaud when we extol the virtues of DIS for training.

DIS is not used to train soldiers how to drive tanks, shoot guns, or load ammunition; or aircrews how to fly airplanes in formation, land airplanes, or conduct dogfights; or sailors how to operate reactors, load torpedoes, or launch aircraft from a catapult. DIS is not intended for training in basic functional skills. Rather, DIS is the place where already trained soldiers earn their Ph.D.'s in warfighting.[9] These graduate studies for warriors in DIS consist of exercising all the elements of human decision making in warfighting—actionable command and control.

DIS lets us hook together the decision-making elements of any battlespace. It lets us build a battlespace filled with human-machine and autonomous simulators of all ilks—airplane, ship, ground vehicle, command post, foxhole, or satellite. DIS lets us pretend to fight the war today with variations of the future on any theme. The significance of DIS is that it is a collection of free-playing, interactive, human-operated elements of the battlespace. This allows for completely unarbitrated free play among the participants, and human decision making directly impacts the outcome of every event.

In the unrefereed, dynamic, "real-time" free play of DIS, actionable command and control is the element of human decision making and interaction in crisis—on the spot, as the battle unfolds, based on the events as they transpire. Decisions whether to drop the bomb, shoot the missile, make the radio call, send the data, shoot the cannon, reallocate the aircraft flight, sacrifice the reconnaissance vehicle, launch the cruise missile, change the target allocations, redirect supplies, forward the intelligence estimate, declare an unknown aircraft hostile or friendly—these are all actionable command and control decisions. It is the human involvement intrinsic to DIS that makes it possible to explore and train for issues in actionable command and control.

The driver for actionable command and control is mastery of the information flow—information dominance. The Department of Defense uses ongoing Advanced Concept Technology Demonstrations to explore these issues. One demonstration, called Battlefield Awareness and Data Dissemination, closely approximates the tenets of information dominance. This program focuses on improving how information is transferred in the battlespace while ensuring that commanders and soldiers are not overwhelmed with the flow of data.[10] DIS provides a mechanism to implement demonstrations such as this and explore actionable command and control.

DIS TRAINING PAYOFF

Traditionally, DIS has been used for training. The Army has used SIMNET (the precursor to DIS) in armor and aviation training simulations since the late 1980s. In the first days of distributed simulation, the Army found that training in SIMNET had a quantifiable payoff.

It was in 1987 that the Army 3rd Armored Division won the coveted Canadian Cup trophy for a mock tank battle in Europe with a record high score—a victory directly attributable to their SIMNET experience. The Canadian Cup battle rules stipulated that as soon as a battleground was selected for the competition, it was sealed off for training before the event. Before SIMNET was fully developed and operational, and years before the concept of DIS was formally articulated, the Army used DIS-like training to practice for the yearly competition. Using SIMNET, the Army developed a computer database simulating the designated 1987 battleground and allowed the tank crews to conduct extensive training on this exact replica of the competition area. When the actual competition was held, members of the 3rd Armored Division swept the game in their M1A1 Abrams tanks, earning 90 percent of the possible points. Even with the ostensibly low fidelity of the SIMNET system, the 3rd Armored Division believed that its training was more than adequate to give the tank crews the competitive edge of feeling as if they had fought there before.

The payoff of simulating the real world and getting the first ten battles under their belts before going to war[11] was further substantiated by the experience of Captain H. R. McMaster in the Battle of 73 Easting. In 1990, the Army's simulators were equipped with a visualization database for Southwest Asia, specifically the Saudi Arabia–Kuwait–Iraq database. A large percentage of the operational personnel for Desert Storm drove and flew through the Iraqi desert long before they deployed to the theater. The training impact was significant. In particular, armor personnel reported that the tactical, command and control, and situational awareness improvements they mastered in the distributed simulation enabled them to sweep through the Iraqi desert without hesitation, as if they were fighting there for the second time.[12] As Captain McMaster and his company members recounted, having fought on the same terrain of the Southwest Asian theater while within SIMNET provided them with the situational awareness and a combat edge that enabled them to overrun a numerically superior Iraqi force.

DIS AS A MEANS OF AMELIORATING
WARFIGHTING DEFICIENCIES

Although DIS is not expected to contribute directly to the fighting of any specific war, it may provide a means of improving our warfighting beyond training. It may let us search for ways to identify and ameliorate our warfighting deficiencies. Future warfighting techniques depend on several key considerations:

- Joint connectivity of systems
- Timeliness and coordination of processes
- Accuracy and currency of information
- Readiness of forces
- Application of appropriate weapons

It is actionable command and control, the human decision-making processes and interactions between each of these elements—the tank commanders, the ship captains, the aircraft pilots, the armor battery commanders, the unmanned air vehicle controllers—that are central to the evolution of DIS for simulation engineering for warfighting.

In December 1994, the late Admiral Jeremy Boorda, as Chief of Naval Operations, spoke to the simulation industry about the new joint roles and missions in the Department of Defense and how simulation was critical to understanding the evolutionary process and changes that were occurring. He stated that "rather than depending on lessons learned . . . simulation technology provides us revolutionary capabilities [to] experiment and test new warfighting concepts . . . anticipated needs and potential technologies." He went on to emphasize that "simulation technology appears to be a viable means to bring the right force into the 21st century."[13] Admiral Boorda typified the sentiment of support for DIS that permeates Department of Defense leadership, looking to DIS to help maintain the readiness of our forces in this time of military downsizing. He made the point that operational demands will continue to grow, even as human and physical resources diminish.

Throughout this era of dwindling resources and increasing operational demands, we have been bombarded with the jointness litany—that all future military operations will be joint. Operation Restore Democracy in Haiti was a sterling example of conceivable future joint combat operations. Could we have imagined that we would have Army helicopter battalions based on and operating from Navy aircraft carriers? The mere thought of such novel joint service operations risks charges of heresy of the grandest sort—a violation of the cultural sanctity of the individual services. But where can such revolutionary jointness doctrines be practiced before implementation? DIS provides an avenue to explore such shifts from traditional operations, at marginal cost and ostensibly no risk. These experiments would be exercises in actionable command and control tested via simulation.

Likewise, a growing tactical necessity for future operations is that U.S. forces must be highly responsive and unambiguous in target selection and execution. Our capabilities rely on improved high-precision conventional munitions that provide results with little or no collateral damage. Our techniques must be employable within the confines of a mixed battlespace, where physical, political, social, and cultural boundaries between friendly and enemy forces are at best dubious and at worst commingled. These dependencies imply a whole slew of new and necessary interactions among all echelons of warfighters—

from the soldier, sailor, and aircrew to the Joint Forces Commander. Deriving the effects of and managing the interactions in actionable command and control, examining the impact of the new technologies involved, and exploring the implications on operations provide the context for the future use of DIS.

DIS DIRECTIONS

Today, advocates of DIS assert that the unique human-machine simulation of combat that DIS provides is useful not only for training but also for research—for example, to assess the effectiveness of proposed tactics or weapons. According to Dr. Anita Jones, former Director of Defense Research and Engineering, "the Department of Defense has long used modeling and simulation tools, traditionally constructive, mathematical, stand-alone models. Advances in information technology offer new opportunities for tools to aid the military analytic community. Of particular potential is distributed simulation."[14] Dr. Jones suggested that the dramatic increase in speed of both computers and network communications makes it timely to ask whether distributed simulation might be a useful tool for military analysts.

However, most admit that it would be prohibitively expensive, for example, to assess the effect of a proposed surveillance system in 1,000 different conditions by putting operational personnel in simulators for 1,000 exercises. Such analytical tasks are usually accomplished by computer-centered simulations that simulate human behavior autonomously, along with other dynamic processes. This allows the computer-centered simulation to run much faster than actual time, so the research can be completed quickly and inexpensively. Of course, the validity of the results depends on the validity of the model of human behavior designed into the simulation. This is not a new issue, nor is it a simulation issue.[15] Clearly, there will always be a place for computer-centered simulations for quantitative analysis. That is not the domain of DIS, nor is it its strength in evaluating actionable command and control.

So what has changed? asked Dr. Jones.[16] Computers and communications are faster—much faster—but they are also more affordable. This enables modelers to use finer grained models that execute in the same elapsed time as older models with less precision did. High-speed communications permit models at remote sites to be run in concert. It is appropriate to ask whether there are situations in which interactive simulations are useful.

Further, Dr. Jones points out that software technology has advanced considerably. Reusability of components allows faster development and more disciplined verification of models and simulations. The training community has developed both virtual and constructive simulations, so that remote sites routinely cooperate in a single simulation. Rich options for user interaction are possible even in simulations executing a scenario in real time or faster than real time. It is becoming possible to link actual operational weapon systems as integral elements in a simulation.

According to a *National Defense* assessment in November 1994, DIS is viewed as the preferred mechanism to achieve joint training objectives at all echelons of the joint warfighting arena.[17] Virtual networks will permit thousands of players around the globe to participate in joint warfighting exercises. That assessment corroborates the decade-long investment in the SIMNET and current DIS efforts. Those investments mitigate a nagging concern for military leaders: that "pressure from the environmentally conscious public also is convincing military staffs that large scale maneuvers with hundreds of vehicles on the ground are a thing of the past."[18]

Since the early 1980s we have experimented with and invested hundreds of millions of dollars in DIS and SIMNET. Interactive simulation technologies have been used extensively in training, particularly by the Army for training armor and aviation units. Recently, DIS has been used by the Air Force and the Navy in experiments such as Zen Regard as a decision-aiding tool to help lower the cost of weapon system acquisition, for force-on-force training exercises, and for large-scale war games with up to 100,000 participants.[19] Our senior leadership has seized upon the idea that the Department of Defense can use simulation to reduce development costs for new systems by evaluating new technologies in battle labs using synthetic environments. Joint warfighting centers have been created for doctrine development and assessment using simulation. By the turn of the century, the Department of Defense will have spent over a billion dollars on DIS. It is a tall order to take a technology created for training (for which it is admittedly well suited) and turn it into the oracle of acquisition wisdom.

As complex as these issues are, DIS projects, by definition, are not meant to stand alone. A long-term concern among the many disparate development communities and members of the government has been that there is little common ground between simulation projects, little to ensure that the final products can collaborate consistently. In 1995, the Defense Advanced Research Projects Agency (DARPA) began a long-term simulation architecture study to determine in what direction Advanced Distributed Simulation should move. The study was passed to the Defense Modeling and Simulation Office, with the objective of defining an architecture to apply within the Department of Defense. The result was the High Level Architecture Baseline Definition, and in September 1996, the Undersecretary of Defense for Acquisition and Technology mandated its adoption for all Department of Defense simulation programs, with an adoption plan required by the summer of 1997 and with compliance required by 1999. In the keynote technical paper introducing the High Level Architecture (HLA), the chief scientist of the Defense Modeling and Simulation Office, Dr. Judith Dahmann, stated that the architecture was "developed to support a broad spectrum of distributed simulation applications, building on the experience of the DIS protocol with extensions to support requirements of an extended set of users of distributed simulation."[20] She further stated that the High Level

Architecture was to provide a Department of Defense–wide common framework to facilitate interoperability and promote reuse of simulations and their components. The paper stated that the establishment of the baseline of HLA would be through the development of a set of prototypes, principal among which was the DIS program Synthetic Theater of War–97. The extensions to DIS to facilitate the High Level Architecture mandate were labeled DIS++, which was a software-culture allusion to the growth of the C programming language into C++.

It is easy to understand how readers might leap to the conclusion that this new High Level Architecture "disconnects" and replaces DIS.[21] The simulation community expressed significant concern regarding the mandate that all Department of Defense simulations be HLA-compliant and members of a "federation" by the year 1999. This caused a financial uproar among managers and users in the simulation community.

However, for the most part, introduction of the High Level Architecture is a paper exercise. It amounts to a process for specifying, developing, testing, and documenting the creation and interaction of simulations. The fundamental underpinnings of simulation—and of DIS, specifically—remain unchanged. Perhaps of equal importance is that understanding the parts of DIS and visualization becomes the linchpin to success within the paradigm of HLA. The 1995–96 study on the use of simulation for acquisition, commissioned by the Director of Test, System Engineering, and Evaluation, determined that the challenge will be to institutionalize modeling and simulation so that it is used productively in an integrated manner in the acquisition process. Articulation of the High Level Architecture is insufficient to guarantee its success. The study found that program managers and their staffs are not well informed on modeling and simulation tools, have had limited exposure to simulation, and would benefit from instruction on modeling and simulation.[22]

This book provides a visceral understanding of the technology of DIS and its tie to the High Level Architecture. It discusses the history of DIS, who the players are, and the philosophy of DIS users. The book defines DIS technology in detail, addresses the importance of visualization for human-centered simulations, examines the use of DIS for training and for acquisition, defines a process for applying DIS as a system engineering tool, and enumerates the new paradigm of the High Level Architecture.

Along the way, the book addresses a number of issues and questions. For example: Is there an analytical process that applies DIS to simulation engineering for warfighting? Can DIS contribute to resolving issues in joint operational doctrine? To pun the issue, is DIS virtually reality, or is Distributed Interactive Simulation just charismatic vaporware consuming the imagination and energy of a new generation of computer-enthralled Department of Defense leaders and managers? Should efforts to apply simulation to acquisition be separate and independent of the already successful training simulation? Or are training simulations by their very nature a more appropriate home for system engineering à la acquisition exploration? Creating synthetic worlds for simulation can be expensive. Are the answers and results worth the investment? Are there overarching problems of warfare that can best—or perhaps only—be solved through the application of DIS? In the end, the book ties together the concepts of information dominance, battlespace dominance, and virtual dominance to provide users and managers with the background they need to determine whether they should invest in DIS at all.

Opinions, conclusions, and recommendations expressed or implied are solely those of the author and do not necessarily represent the views of the Department of Defense or any other U.S. government agency. Information presented is from public sources, especially the World Wide Web, without which this work would not have been possible.

1

What Is Distributed Interactive Simulation?

Is Distributed Interactive Simulation a technology, a product that can be purchased in a shrink-wrapped box?[23] Is it a process or methodology for conducting simulation? Is it a physical network of interconnected sites around the world? Is it a specification defining integration among disparate simulation devices? Is it a real-time database communication approach? Perhaps the answer is a resounding yes to each question. Distributed Interactive Simulation is all these things and more. As one DIS software engineer adroitly obfuscated the issue:

> The powerful functionality of Distributed Interactive Simulation can be summed up as massively distributed databases communicating asynchronously with time-sensitive information across choked flow network conduits in people-intensive tasks.[24]

This definition of DIS is not particularly enlightening. The official Institute of Electrical and Electronics Engineers (IEEE) definition is no more succinct:

> Distributed Interactive Simulation (DIS). A time and space coherent synthetic representation of world environments designed for linking the interactive, free-play activities of people in operational exercises. The synthetic environment is created through real-time exchange of data units between distributed, computationally autonomous simulation applications in the form of simulations, simulators, and instrumented equipment interconnected through standard computer communicative services. The computational simulation entities may be present in one location or may be distributed geographically.[25]

So what is it that makes DIS fundamentally different from any other simulation domain? There is no simple, plain-English, one-sentence definition for

DIS. Definition by example is more instructive. Certainly what is most noticeable about DIS is its ability to connect widely varying types of simulators scattered around the world. For example, during the Zen Regard exercises in 1993, a DIS synthetic environment of fifty different types of simulators was created (see Figure 1).

Each simulator was able to fly, drive, float, and fight in the same virtual battlespace (Southwest Asia), with participants able to see one another and the enemy as appropriate. Few, if any, of these simulators were originally intended or designed to interact with one another electronically. DIS provided the mechanization that made the joint battlespace possible. According to the Institute for Simulation and Training, the challenge "is to arrive at a method of networking different simulators which will allow realistic simulation exercises to be held on hardware of varying design while insuring that the different simulators interact with each other in a manner that allows a 'fair fight.'"[26]

To understand DIS in total, and how exercises like Zen Regard are possible, it is essential to grasp some of the underpinning technologies. Although it would be inappropriate to attempt to condense volumes of graduate electrical engineering into these pages, a modicum of engineering jargon must be laid out. The essential subjects for a bare-bones understanding of DIS include:

- The distinctions among live, virtual, and constructive simulations
- The issues and meanings of timeliness, entities, and granularity
- A perspective on virtual reality versus virtual simulation
- The simulation parts that make up DIS

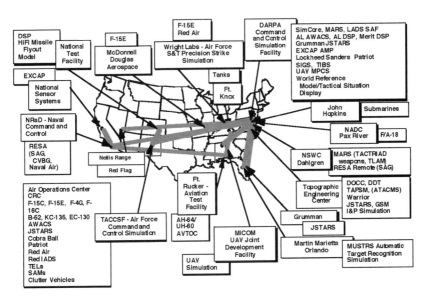

Figure 1. Zen Regard Simulation Systems

- The structure of DIS operations
- The networking fundamentals that make DIS possible

Volumes have been written elsewhere on each of these subjects, as cited in the notes.

LIVE, VIRTUAL, AND CONSTRUCTIVE SIMULATION

Bounding Distributed Interactive Simulation and coming to terms with what DIS actually is can be a tortuous process. There is no easy way to convey a useful understanding of DIS without delving into the technical complexity of the subject. As a first step in discussing DIS, consider the following canonical definitions from Department of Defense Directive 5000.59, intended to clarify the distinction between the terms *modeling* and *simulation:*[27]

> Model: A physical, mathematical, or otherwise logical representation of a system, entity, phenomenon, or process.

> Simulation: A method for implementing a model over time. Also, a technique for testing, analysis, or training in which real-world systems are used, or where real-world and conceptual systems are reproduced by a model.

With these two definitions in mind, and recalling General Gorman's thesis that anything that isn't war is simulation, consider the three descriptors that people commonly apply to simulation: live, virtual, and constructive. In their simplest form, they are distinguished by their physical manifestations or lack thereof. Live simulation is centered around using real-world equipment, such as airplanes, tanks, and ships, and playing at war, as opposed to actually fighting it. Virtual simulation can also be thought of as playing at war, but people are inside simulators rather than actual equipment. Constructive simulation usually consists of computerized models of people and machines playing at war inside a computer program. In each of these simulation domains, the individual airplanes, tanks, ships, and people are referred to as entities. It is the relative detail of each entity that characterizes the nature of the simulation. Entities in live simulation are real-world things, such as machines and people. Entities in virtual simulation are typically models of machines and people, each model being independent and interactive. Entities in constructive simulation tend to be subsumed into larger groupings of things, such as tank battalions, aircraft flights, and naval fleets. DIS is considered to be virtual simulation of combat.

The theme of this text is to capture the essence of virtual combat as realizable in DIS. By its evolving nature, DIS may contain other elements of both live and constructive simulation, but it principally entails the technologies and techniques of creating and peopling virtual worlds. It is important, however, to recognize the distinctions across the spectrum of live, virtual, and constructive simulation, as pictured in Figure 2.

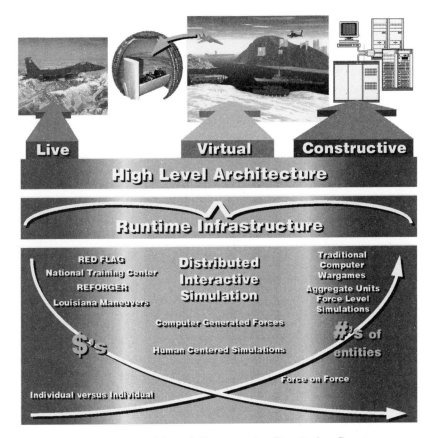

Figure 2. The Live-Virtual-Constructive Simulation Spectrum

Live simulation is very clear-cut, as characterized by activities that utilize actual hardware and personnel. Examples of live simulation are tank drivers driving M1A1 Abrams tanks around training ranges, pilots flying air-to-air intercept missions during Top Gun or Red Flag missions, and captains steaming their ships in fleet exercises. It can mean a single operator with a single weapon system, or it can be massed forces in traditional training activities, such as the annual Reforger exercise or the time-honored Louisiana Maneuvers of the World War II era.

Constructive simulation is most commonly thought of as the classic studies and analysis, war-gaming, and statistical and logistical models that have forever run from card decks on mainframes in the back room of every organization that ever had a computer. Constructive simulations typically involve aggregate units (companies or battalions, squadrons or wings), run at or faster than real time, and play large-scale scenarios (on the corps, division, wing, or task-force level). Today, constructive simulation is quite sophisticated but retains the key feature of not directly supporting interactive, dynamic free play, particularly of the sort deemed actionable command and control. Constructive simulation executes courses of events that are initiated by controlled sets of inputs. Human intervention is minimal.

Constructive simulation and its variants generally are used to model macroprocesses. Examples are too numerous to list here. Many constructive simulations also contribute to the planning and execution of DIS exercises and should be used in any system engineering process using DIS. Some typical examples of these are discussed in Appendix B, including the Rapid Scenario Preparation Unit for Intelligence (RASPUTIN), the Conventional Targeting Effectiveness Model (CTEM), the Extended Air Defense Simulation (EADSIM), the Exercise Capability simulator (EXCAP), the Joint Modeling and Simulation System (J-MASS), the Multiwarfare Assessment and Research System (MARS), the Research, Evaluation, and Systems Analysis system (RESA), and SimCore.[28]

TIMELINESS, ENTITIES, AND GRANULARITY

The definition of *simulation* states that it is "a method for implementing a model over time." Stepping back for a moment, consider the phrase "over time." It implies that a simulation represents a system, entity, phenomenon, or process that changes with time. The simulation implements a model that predicts intermediate conditions that are expected to occur over the span of time between the starting condition and the final time. However, not all models are dynamic. Constructive combat models typically predict which side will win a battle or how many soldiers and vehicles will survive, based on the numbers and types of units committed to battle when it begins. This prediction is made without estimating how the situation might change during the battle.

In virtual simulations, in contrast, we see how an initial situation may change in countless ways during a battle by observing human participants making decisions and plans, issuing orders, operating sensors, or pulling triggers. These were formerly called man-in-the-loop simulations. In this text they are called human-machine simulations or, if no computer is involved, human-centered simulations, in accordance with Institute of Electrical and Electronic Engineers (IEEE) Standard 610.3.[29] DIS human-machine simulation is especially characterized by dynamic free play. The actionable command and control element of DIS is manifested by the interactive actions, reactions, planning, and decision making of the DIS participants.

Simulations and models can also be classified on the basis of their time scales. Real-time simulations operate with events occurring at the same rate as the corresponding real-world events. Non-real-time simulations operate faster or slower than real time. Certainly, simulations expected to examine thousands of test cases would best be run at faster than real time, if we ever hoped to get useful quantitative measurements out of them. DIS is a real-time simulation—one minute on the proverbial wall clock takes exactly one minute in a DIS simulation. So one of the strengths of DIS—the real-time interaction of human players—poses a potential liability if we have to perform multiple iterations of the same experiment.

Continuing along that vein, computer-based battlespace simulations and models can be divided into two broad classes, based on the granularity of the entities being simulated or modeled, called *aggregate* (constructive) and *entity level* (virtual). The granularity is the level of detail or delineation of discernible differences between individual things being modeled. Aggregate simulations control units (e.g,. the tanks in a tank company) as a whole rather than simulating each individual entity within the unit. The position, movement, status, and composition of aggregate units are maintained for the unit as a whole and are the result of statistical analysis of the unit's actions rather than the result of the actions of the individual entities. In contrast, entity-level simulations represent each vehicle as a distinct simulation entity. The position, movement, status, and composition of units in entity-level simulations are inferred directly from the individual entities. Computer-supported war games and Distributed Interactive Simulations are typically aggregate and entity-level simulations, respectively.[30] Constructive battlefield simulations typically control groups of entities (e.g., the tanks in a tank company) as an aggregate rather than as a set of individual simulated entities. In contrast, virtual simulations represent vehicles (e.g., tanks) as distinct simulation entities within a common simulated (or virtual) environment.[31]

The issues of timescales and entity definitions would not be worth mentioning if it were not for the desirability of interconnecting various simulations. Interconnection implies interoperability. The differences in entity granularity and timescales create difficulties in simulation interoperability. For example, in the battlefield environment, it is difficult for entities in entity-level simulations to detect and react to aggregate units from constructive simulations. Similarly, units in aggregate simulations typically do not detect and attack individual virtual-simulation entities. The problems associated with differing timescales are obvious; simulations need to be operating at the same timescale for their interactions to make sense. This challenge has been tackled again and again, each time a major new simulation experiment has been undertaken.[32]

VIRTUAL REALITY?

Virtual simulation brings to mind the term *virtual reality*. Virtual reality is the popular name for a new form of absorbing, interactive, computer-mediated experience characterized by the participant's unawareness of the artificiality of the experience.[33] A recent NASA report offered this definition: "Virtual reality is the human experience of perceiving and interacting through sensors and effectors with a synthetic (simulated) environment, and with simulated objects in it, as if they were real."[34] Some pundits object to the term virtual reality, saying that it is an oxymoron. Other terms that have been used are synthetic environments, cyberspace, artificial reality, and simulator technology. In general, the DIS community disowns the term virtual reality and prefers the terms *synthetic environment* and *virtual simulation.*

In virtual simulation, the participant performs tasks in an environment that is altered or replicated to some extent by combinations of computer hardware, software, and perception systems. This does not mean virtual reality per se. In the case of a motion-base dome simulator, the actual cockpit may be borrowed from a flight-worthy airplane, placed on hydraulic suspension that is computer actuated, and surrounded with a computer graphics visual dome. The other extreme of virtual simulation might be an aircrew member sitting in front of a desktop computer with joysticks flying the latest release of an F/A-18 game. In fact, if these two virtual simulations were networked together, neither participant could tell that the other was flying either a dome or a desktop simulator. The primary difference for the participants is the "realism" or level of immersion felt in their use of a particular simulation. The key to virtual simulation is that participants take an active and decisive part in the real-time flow of activities. This is representative of actionable command and control.

Although the Department of Defense is currently preoccupied with DIS and virtual simulation, our exposure to interactive simulation is decades old. Virtual simulation comes in various shades of gray—that is, various approximations of reality. It is most obvious when considering recent examples, such as expensive motion-base dome simulators for fighter aircraft. But one of the early noteworthy examples of virtual simulation was the introduction of the Link Trainer in 1929. It consisted of a mock-up of an aircraft cockpit balanced on top of a gimbaled base. It was used to teach pilots "blind flying" or flying with only cockpit instruments. The first of these Link Trainers was sold to the Navy in 1931 for $1,500. Interestingly, of the first fifty-three Link Trainers sold by mid-1932, fifty were sold for use in amusement parks—a trend paralleling today's entertainment demand for the high-fidelity simulation techniques developed for warfighting simulation. The attraction of virtual simulation among the Department of Defense, industry, and the public is that the participant is absorbed into the interactive experience.

An early example in the development of DIS-like simulations was the technology demonstrator for the U.S. Air Force air defense program called SAGE. In creating a System Training Program for SAGE, in the 1950s the Air Force built what today would be called a virtual human-machine distributed interactive simulation, in which radar operators and weapon controllers reacted to simulated targets presented to them as real targets would be in war. This was relatively easy to do, since the human-computer interface was only a radar screen. In contrast, today's problem of presenting a tank gunner or a fighter pilot with a detailed, rapidly changing visual scene requires radical advances in computer image generation technology.

One of the features of SAGE was the extensive use of simulation programs and operational testing aids; the System Training Program created simulated airplanes by signals entered into the system at the radar sites. These and other simulated inputs were integrated to create a simulated scenario against which the operators could direct intercepts and be scored on their performance. In this system, an internal program simulated airplane signals that could be mixed with live signals generated by real aircraft. The SAGE system later pioneered the networking of two collocated computers for reliability and eventually the networking of remote computers for distributed computing—in a real sense, manifesting the first distributed interactive live and virtual simulations.[35]

THE PIECES OF DIS

In the early 1980s the categorization of live, virtual, or constructive simulation did not exist. The dawn of distributed simulation occurred well before the image of virtual reality was generated. Distributed simulation was given birth in a collaborative program between the Defense Advanced Research Projects Agency (DARPA)[36] and the Army, in a program called Simulator Network, or SIMNET. The framework of SIMNET, and the lessons learned from it, led to the development and implementation of DIS as a Department of Defense and industry standard for simulation.

The principles first demonstrated by the Air Force in the 1950s in SAGE have advanced a long way in hardware and software to become DIS. Consider the building blocks of DIS: host computers, simulation applications, simulation entities, simulation exercises, simulation environments, and DIS Protocol Data Units (see Figure 3). Each of these elements is an essential piece that makes DIS possible.

Principal Elements

In one sense, DIS consists merely of collections of host computers operating together, supporting one or more simulation applications simultaneously. These host computers participating in simulation exercises are connected by common high-speed computer communication networks.

The simulation applications for DIS are the executing software on the host computers (or simulators) that generate one or more simulation entities. For example, an F-15E fighter aircraft simulator can be considered a host computer executing one simulation application and generating one entity (itself). Each simulation application represents or simulates real-world phenomena for the purpose of training or experimentation. Other examples of simulation applications include manned vehicle simulators, computer-generated aggregate forces, and computer interfaces between a DIS network and real equipment. Each simulation application receives and processes information concerning entities created by its other peer simulation applications (simulation applications on other host computers) through the exchange of DIS Protocol Data Units (PDUs). In addition, more than one simulation application may be executed simultaneously on a particular host computer.

A simulation entity is an element of the synthetic environment that is

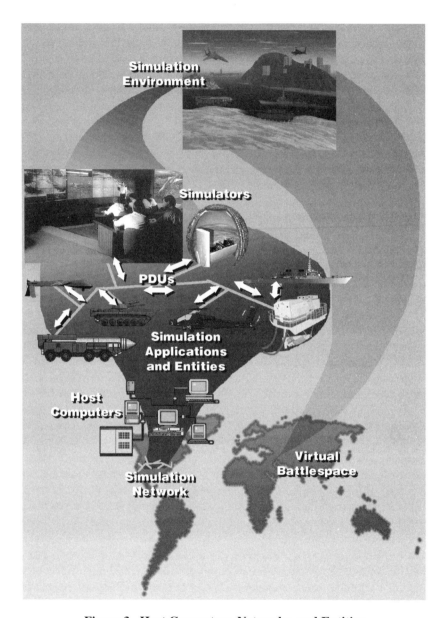

Figure 3. Host Computers, Networks, and Entities

created and controlled by a simulation application on a host computer through the exchange of DIS PDUs. Examples of simulated entities are individual personnel, tanks, submarines, carriers, fighter aircraft, missiles, bridges, or other elements of the synthetic environment. It is possible for a simulation application to be controlling more than one simulation entity. Simulation entities are also referred to simply as entities.

A simulation exercise consists of one or more interacting simulation applications across multiple host computers on a common network. Simulations participating in the same simulation exercise share a common identifying number called the Exercise Identifier.

A simulation environment consists of the operational environment surrounding the simulation entities. This environment includes terrain, atmospheric, and bathyspheric information. Simulation entities fly and fight in the same synthetic world by utilizing correlated representations of the simulation environment in which they operate.

DIS Protocol Data Units

The single, most fundamental building block of DIS is the Protocol Data Unit (PDU). All of DIS is centered around the transmission, receipt, and processing of PDUs. PDUs constitute discrete messages between simulation applications that describe the actions and the current state of all simulation entities. Simulation applications typically transmit PDUs describing their own entities at rates varying from fifteen times per second to as infrequently as once every thirty seconds. The receipt and processing of PDUs make it possible for unrelated but interconnected simulators to see and fight with each other in the virtual world.

The PDU distributed-message-passing-protocol architecture makes simulation interoperability feasible. The participating simulators are all real-time simulators, and the DIS exchanges are conducted in real time as well. Individual simulators locally provide the computing capability to represent detailed aspects of their internal characteristics and the ability to exchange public information about changes in their state and events with external consequences. Each simulator also maintains a local or dead-reckoning model of itself (see the later discussion) and all other platforms in the shared battlespace to support continuous interaction among objects between message exchanges. Interaction is based on the broadcast of messages, with individual simulators responding to those messages with local impact.[37]

There are twenty-seven different PDU types, divided into six PDU families (see Table 1). In addition to these PDUs associated with DIS applications, PDU types and protocol families have been reserved for PDU growth so that others can be added to the standard in the future. PDU types and protocol families in the range of 129 through 255 are reserved for experimental purposes.

A typical PDU is the Entity State PDU, essential to all entity simulations. Table 2 describes its content.

DIS STRUCTURE

Each of the elements discussed earlier contributes to DIS characterization as a virtual simulation. Yet even though the domains of live, virtual, and constructive simulation are well defined and understood, there is still debate about

TABLE 1: PROTOCOL DATA UNITS (PDUS)

1. **Entity Information/Interaction**
   Entity State PDU
   Collision PDU
2. **Warfare**
   Fire PDU
   Detonation PDU
3. **Logistics**
   Service Request PDU
   Resupply Offer PDU
   Resupply Received PDU
   Resupply Cancel PDU
   Repair Complete PDU
   Repair Response PDU
4. **Simulation Management**
   Start/Resume PDU
   Stop/Freeze PDU
   Acknowledge PDU
   Action Request PDU
   Action Response PDU
   Data Query PDU
   Set Data PDU
   Data PDU
   Event Report PDU
   Message PDU
   Create Entity PDU
   Remove Entity PDU
5. **Distributed Emission Regeneration**
   ElectroMagnetic Emission PDU
   Designator PDU
6. **Radio Communications**
   Transmitter PDU
   Signal PDU
   Receiver PDU

where on the spectrum of simulation domains a particular simulation falls. With the growth of DIS, simulations have begun to migrate across the boundaries. A number of projects discussed later have blurred the distinction by cross-coupling and integrating simulations from all three domains. It is its underlying structure that makes DIS uniquely evolutionary.

DIS expands on the precepts established by the SIMNET program as originally developed by DARPA. The basic concepts for SIMNET, and now DIS and HLA, are:

- No central computer controls the entire simulation exercise.
- Autonomous simulation applications are responsible for maintaining the state of one or more simulation entities.
- A standard protocol is used for communicating "ground truth" data.
- Changes in the state of an entity are communicated by simulation applications.
- Perception of events or other entities is determined by the receiving application.
- Dead-reckoning algorithms are used to reduce communications processing.

TABLE 2: ENTITY STATE PDU

- Identification of the entity that issued the PDU.
- Identification of the force to which the entity belongs.
- The issuing entity's specific entity type.
- The issuing entity's alternate entity type for use with the Guise function.
- Information about the location of the entity in the simulated world and its orientation. This information includes:
    Location with respect to the world.
    Velocity (the rate at which its location is changing).
    Orientation.
    The dead-reckoning parameters that should be employed when extrapolating the position of this entity. Values in this field include the dead-reckoning algorithm in use, linear acceleration, and angular velocity. Other values for this field are currently undefined.
- The information required for representation of the entity's visual appearance. This information includes:
    The appearance of the entity (for example, normal, smoking, on fire, producing a dust cloud).
    Markings.
    The number of articulation parameters and the parameter values to represent orientation of articulated parts.
    The presence of attached parts or stores.
- The capabilities of the entity. Defined capabilities include:
    Resupply.
    Repair.

No Central Computer

Some war games have a central computer that maintains the world state and calculates the effects of each entity's actions on other entities and the environment. These computer systems must be sized with resources to handle the worst caseload for a maximum number of simulated entities. DIS uses a distributed computing approach in which the responsibility for simulating the state of each entity rests with separate simulation applications residing in host computers connected via a common network. As new host computers are added to the network, each new host computer brings its own computational resources.

Autonomous Simulation Applications

Simulation applications are autonomous and are generally responsible for maintaining the state of one entity. In some cases, a simulation application is responsible for maintaining the state of several entities. As the user operates controls in the simulated or actual equipment, the simulation application is responsible for modeling the resulting actions of the entity using a high-fidelity simulation model. That simulation application is responsible for sending messages to others, as necessary, to inform them of any observable actions. All simulation applications are responsible for interpreting and responding to messages of interest from other simulation applications and maintaining a model of the state of entities represented in the simulation exercise. Simulation applications may also maintain a model of the state of the environment and nondynamic entities, such as bridges and buildings, that may be intact or destroyed.

Ground Truth versus Perception

Each simulation application communicates the state of the entity it controls (location, orientation, velocity, articulated parts position, and so forth) to other simulation applications on the network. The receiving simulation application is responsible for taking this ground truth data and calculating whether the entity represented by the sending simulation application is detectable by visual or electronic means. This perceived state of the entity is then displayed to the user as required by the individual simulation application.

State Vectors

In DIS, a simulator models the behavior of an entity in real time and communicates the current status of that entity to other entities in the synthetic environment. DIS is a four-dimensional problem domain, concerned with the three dimensions of space and the fourth dimension of time. Entities are seldom static. An entity has a state vector—location (x, y, x), orientation (roll, pitch, yaw), and velocity (v_x, v_y, v_z), as shown in Figure 4—which may be constantly changing. The simulator modeling the entity must inform other simulators of changes in the state vector so that all the simulators participating in an exercise can depict the entity correctly at its current location, orientation, and velocity.

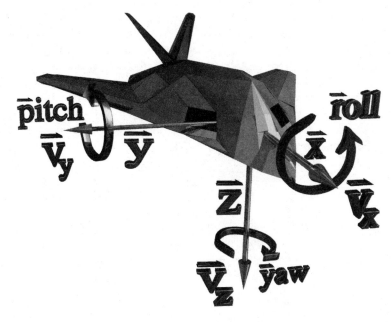

Figure 4. Components of the Simulation State Vector

With a large number of simulators needing to send their location, orientation, and velocity information, the network traffic load can be overwhelming.

Perception
DIS relies on the ability of each end user to process the simulation environment and recreate the events and entities around it. Each application must build its own awareness of the world in which it resides. It is the application's responsibility to manifest its world in a fashion in concert with the ground truth, the changes in entity states and the algorithms of the other entities and applications. This manifestation is the application's perception of the simulation environment. For each simulation, its perception is its own definition of reality. The wide variety of simulation applications and the hardware on which they run causes there to be an extreme spread in the possible nature of perception. This topic merits significant further discussion and is covered in detail in Chapter 2.

Dead Reckoning
To minimize the need to send information, a common method is used to estimate and update position and orientation. It is called Dead Reckoning. The term, borrowed from navigation, refers to establishing the position of a ship by using an earlier known position and estimating time and motion since that position. For DIS, the method limits the rate at which simulation applications must

issue state vector updates for their entities. Simulators may use Dead Reckoning to extrapolate the changing state vectors of all entities, thus reducing the frequency with which they have to obtain the actual information from the network.[38] Dead Reckoning thus limits the rate at which Entity State PDUs are issued in a simulation exercise. By using Dead Reckoning, simulation applications are not required to broadcast the status of their entities continuously.

High- and Low-Fidelity Models. In Dead Reckoning, each simulation application maintains a high-fidelity model of the entity it represents. In addition, the simulation application maintains a simpler, lower-fidelity dead-reckoning model of its entity. The simpler model represents the view of that entity by other simulation applications on the network and is an extrapolation of position and orientation using a specified dead-reckoning algorithm. Certain thresholds are established as criteria for determining whether the entity's actual position and orientation have varied an allowable amount from its dead-reckoned position and orientation. On a regular basis, the simulation application compares the high-fidelity model of its entity with the simpler model of the entity. When the entity's actual position and orientation have varied from the dead-reckoned position and orientation by more than a threshold value, the simulation application issues an Entity State PDU. This communicates the entity's actual position and orientation to other simulation applications on the network so that they can update their own models of the entity. The simulation application also updates its simpler dead-reckoning model using the information from its high-fidelity model. In Dead Reckoning, the default value for position threshold is one meter, and the default value for orientation threshold is three degrees.

Other Entities. In addition to keeping track of itself, each simulation application maintains dead-reckoning models of the position and orientation of other entities that are of interest to it (i.e., within sight or range). The dead-reckoned position and orientation of other entities are used to display their position and orientation in a simulator's visual or sensor displays. When the simulation application receives a new update from one of the entities it is dead reckoning, it corrects its own dead-reckoning model for that entity and bases its estimations on the most recent position, orientation, velocity, and acceleration information. Numerical smoothing techniques are used to eliminate jitter and jumps that occur in visual displays when the dead-reckoned position and orientation of entities are corrected using more recent position and orientation data.[39]

Scalability. The DIS protocol requires every entity in a simulation to broadcast certain changes (e.g., in its velocity) to every other entity in the simulation ("on the net"). In most cases, however, information such as an airplane's change in heading may be needed only by entities within a 100-kilometer radius in the simulated world. In other instances—for example, if someone wants to connect an over-the-horizon radar simulator to the net to see how much it would influence combat—heading and other information would be needed from aircraft halfway around the simulated world. The DIS protocol requires all entities to broadcast certain information rather than have special broadcast clauses for all the combinations of fighters, helicopters, over-the-horizon radars, and other entities that one can imagine. The approach has worked well to date, but that does not mean that it will work at all if the number of entities in the simulation is increased 100-fold.[40] The issue has raised serious concerns in the DIS community over the scalability of DIS to ever larger simulation environments.

In an example of scale similar to Zen Regard, if 5,000 entities are on the net, and if each makes three reportable changes per minute (taking into account dead-reckoning averages of twenty seconds between updates), then each of the 5,000 entities will be receiving 14,997 (roughly 15,000) messages per minute. If the number of entities on the net is increased to 100,000, then each of 100,000 entities would receive and process 300,000 messages per minute. The aggregate network communications capacity (bandwidth) servicing the entities would likewise need to increase in proportion to the square of the number of entities, and the marginal cost of adding one more simulator to the network would begin to increase approximately in proportion to the square of the number of simulators already on the network. There is also the problem of nonscalability in configuration control. The software for each type of entity (e.g., vehicle or weapon) must be modified when one new type of entity is allowed in the simulation. Thus, there is a limit on the number of entities that can be netted economically, and there is a limit on the number that can be netted at all, although technological advances are constantly increasing these limits.

NETWORKING: PUTTING THE PIECES TOGETHER
If there is any single identifiable technology that makes DIS possible, it is the electronic connection of different computers at different places, known as networking. Simulators have run on computers since the first vacuum tube computer was fabricated. It is the use of networks that allows computers to talk to one another and that makes it possible for simulations to communicate among themselves. Initially, computers were connected locally to provide for common use of shared resources, such as printers and data storage devices (such as tape drives). Networks were built primarily within research and educational organizations. In the 1970s, DARPA pursued technology to extend local-area networking connectivity to wide-area network connectivity between government and academic institutions. Dubbed the ARPANET, this grew unbounded from tens of computers in the United States in the 1970s to tens of millions of computers around the world in the 1990s. Along the way, ARPANET evolved into the Internet.[41]

Packets
Since the early days of computers and networks, it was recognized that if all data from one location were sent to another in one burst, something could get lost or broken along the way. In addition, hardware limits on the speed of data transmission and the devices' ability to talk and listen at both ends encouraged

users to break up large chunks of data into smaller chunks for transmission. This enabled all users of a shared network to trade off time utilization of the sending and receiving capabilities of the network. Formalized, these smaller chunks of data became known as packets. They typically range in size from 1 to 1,500 bytes.

Internet Protocol

Data being transported from one computer to another need to know where to go, how to get there, and when they have arrived. Networks provide the transportation medium by wire, fiber-optic, or electromagnetic means. But the data do not know where to go without help. The Internet Protocol (IP) provides the scheme that has been almost universally adapted for addressing computer communications. IP addresses are the electronic equivalent of postal-mail addresses.[42] The conventional practice is to assign a unique IP address to every device connected to a network. These are likened to post office box numbers, apartment or house numbers, city, state, and country. By convention, an IP address consists of four numbers, each less than 256, separated by periods[43]— for example, 131.84.1.7 or 132.170.193.21. The IP address is a community-assigned artifact used as the standard label among all devices on a network.

Transmission Control Protocol

Transmission Control Protocol (TCP), often mentioned in conjunction with IP, is the mastermind behind the successful delivery of large chunks of data from one address to another across a network. Just as you would be disappointed in a postal system that limited paper mail to postcards, most computer information transfers are longer than 1,500 characters, which is generally all that can be contained in one network packet. And although a postal system may occasionally lose, damage, or significantly delay delivery of a letter, a computer network should be able to handle delivery successfully. TCP subdivides information into packets, numbers them for correct reassembly, and encloses them in its own labeled envelopes for insertion in an IP packet for transmission. Figure 5 depicts two notional local-area networks using TCP to pass IP packets, connected through a notional satellite wide-area network.

The use of TCP creates the appearance of a dedicated network between the sending and receiving computers. It provides high reliability and accuracy for data exchange. All transmitted data are guaranteed to be received exactly as sent. This reliability is the equivalent of sending registered, return-receipt mail every time you send a postcard. Thus, in some cases, it may consume an excessive amount of resources and time.

User Datagram Protocol

A poor cousin to TCP is the User Datagram Protocol (UDP). For smaller information exchanges, in which all the data fit into one packet (1,500 bytes or less), and when it is not particularly important if the information gets through or not,

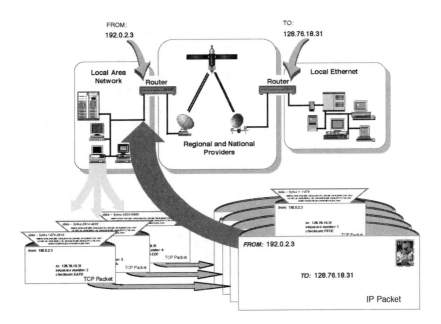

Figure 5. Networks and Packets

UDP is a simpler and more efficient transmission protocol. Each UDP packet is complete unto itself and is contained in an IP envelope. No consideration is given to sending packets in a particular order or to guaranteeing receipt. UDP was intended for information exchanges of short messages, that the sender could simply send again if necessary. In contrast to TCP, in which processing time is spent on both the sender's and the receiver's end in subdividing and then rearranging data, UDP directly packages and unpackages the information, increasing the potential efficiency of the information exchange. UDP was used as the network communication paradigm in the original design of SIMNET.

Domain Name System

It is readily apparent that dealing with IP addresses is something best left to the hardware of computers. People prefer to deal with names. Computers on networks have been given names for the convenience of their users. Nearly all networked computers can be accessed via a name in place of the IP address. With networked computers numbering 100 million or more, keeping track of the names required the development of a naming structure and system. The Domain Name System administers networked computer names by giving different groups responsibility for subsets of names. Similar to IP addresses, the names are words strung together with periods—for example, godsivu.wb.com, tiig.ist.ucf.edu, whitehouse.gov, dmso.mil, ida.org, or cerf.net.

Each word in the name is considered a domain. The first word is usually

TABLE 3: U.S. TOP LEVEL DOMAIN NAMES [44]

Domain	Usage Organizations
com	business and commercial
edu	universities, schools, educational
gov	non-military government
mil	army, navy, air force, and so forth
org	other
net	network resources

the actual name of a physical computer with a real IP address. Each subsequent word is the descriptor of a group or organization under which that computer is maintained, at respectively higher organizational levels. The last (rightmost) name is drawn from the list of six original top-level domains that were created by fiat when the domain system was invented (see Table 3).

Defense Simulation Internet
Networked Department of Defense simulations ranging from the early System Training Program of SAGE to those of SIMNET have used the public telephone network for long-haul connectivity from one location to another. Today, a variety of other networks are also used, including ad hoc local-area networks, the Internet, and the Defense Simulation Internet.

The Defense Simulation Internet is a wide-area network connecting sites worldwide via combinations of dedicated digital communication landlines.[45] It was originally known as the Terrestrial Wide Band Network and was part of the North Atlantic Treaty Organization's (NATO's) Distributed Wargaming System. It was sponsored by DARPA and by NATO's supreme allied commander—Europe. The Terrestrial Wide Band Network was orphaned briefly after the cold war ended but was later adopted by NATO's Warrior Preparation Center, DARPA's SIMNET project, the Department of Defense's Joint Warfighting Center, and the Walker Simulation Center in the Republic of Korea. The Defense Simulation Internet has grown to over 100 nodes (Figure 6)[46] and is now being transferred from DARPA, which developed the technology, to the Defense Information Systems Agency, which will be responsible for it when it is fully operational.

The Defense Simulation Internet was conceived as a DARPA project in the 1980s as an adjunct to the intrafacility local-area networks of SIMNET, providing long-haul connectivity between the original SIMNET sites. It was envisioned as analogous to the ARPANET, which was started by DARPA in the 1970s to provide intercomputer connectivity between universities and eventu-

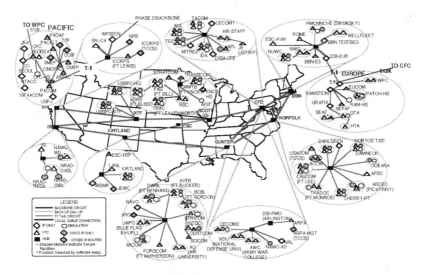

Figure 6. The Defense Simulation Internet

ally grew to become the Internet. The Defense Simulation Internet was built to create a simulator communication conduit.[47] It originally consisted of three primary backbones, two in the United States and one in Europe. The European network was tied to the U.S. network via a 256-kilobits-per-second transatlantic line. The U.S. backbones between Norfolk, Virginia, and Menlo Park, California, ran northern and southern routes. Seventy-three U.S. sites were interconnected via the U.S. backbones, each at what is known as "T-1" communications rates of 1.544-megabits-per-second. An additional eighteen sites were connected overseas. The guiding principle behind connection to the Defense Simulation Internet was conformance to standards for distributed simulation. This required each simulation node to:

• Exist autonomously (no reliance on the existence or presence of any other node).

• Utilize object- and event-based simulation, ground truth, and state-change broadcast methods.

• Use dead-reckoning techniques to compute state changes in order to reduce the data transmission requirements of each user.

In the years since its initiation, the Defense Simulation Internet (together with other networks) has linked heterogeneous simulators in exercises that have included engagements of simulated tanks, other armored vehicles, ships, helicopters, fixed-wing aircraft, cruise missiles, and teams of Marines equipped with laser designators to designate targets for Air Force aircraft equipped with laser-guided bombs. Simulators physically located in the continental United States, Germany, and Republic of Korea have participated in the same exercises, operating in the same virtual battlespace. The Defense Simulation Internet is also used for video teleconferencing in support of traditional war-gaming, as well as for Distributed Interactive Simulation.

The Defense Simulation Internet originally used UDP and IP to package and transmit simulation data. By 1993, the lessons learned over the years caused its management to reexamine UDP use, as opposed to industry-standard TCP and IP techniques. As in any DARPA program, the Defense Simulation Internet was an evolving infrastructure, and continues to mature with the rapid progress in commercial communication technology. The Department of Defense has used, and will continue to use, the rapidly growing commercial, academic, and nonmilitary government networks, such as those that are part of the Internet, for wide-area networking.[48]

The Department of Defense currently pays for the Defense Simulation Internet communications infrastructure and service required to link simulators with low latency—that is, the ability to transmit and receive data between locations with minimal time lag. Access to the Defense Simulation Internet costs $150,000 to $300,000 per node per year. Recently, commercial Internet access providers have been publicly debating the merits of charging for data transfer in dollars per bit—rather than for access privilege, as in the Defense Simulation Internet—depending on the availability required by users and the latency that their data can tolerate. If novel new pricing schemes are adopted, the Department of Defense might be able to pay only for the connectivity, bandwidth, and availability that it requires, for example, during exercises. However, the Department of Defense will most likely maintain some dedicated links, but perhaps fewer as a proportion of the whole. Beginning in 1994, the Defense Simulation Internet started the multiyear transition from DARPA to the Defense Information Systems Agency for its maintenance and operation as a Department of Defense asset.

Concerns. Over the years, one of the issues nagging at the Defense Simulation Internet has been that it is merely a wide-area backbone to carry data long-haul or interstate distances, with little or no provision for local-area connectivity. In fact, the Industry and Department of Defense Steering Committee for Distributed Interactive Simulation reported that the primary bottleneck for Defense Simulation Internet simulations has been local-area networking—the connection of simulators to others nearby and to wide-area network nodes.[49] This concern is compounded by the ominous challenge of building an adequate end-to-end data communications infrastructure. It requires networks to connect all the simulators (as well as any real vehicles, weapons, and other systems) that will be participating in a simulation. It must be capable of transferring enormous quantities of information at rates that will grow at least in proportion to the number of participating entities (simulators and so forth). But with the advent and availability of commercial network providers, the networks do not necessarily need to be dedicated to virtual combat. As noted in the Office of

Technology Assessment report on combat simulation,[50] nondedicated commercial networks will continue to complement the Defense Simulation Internet. The nondedicated networks can be shared with other users and used for other tasks. Improvement of networking protocols can reduce the network bandwidth required for Department of Defense simulations and other uses, and proposed Internet usage-pricing schemes may allow the Department of Defense to pay for only the low latency it needs for simulations.

Encryption Issues. In the Department of Defense, where secure simulation is often a necessity, the biggest problem on the Defense Simulation Internet has been the encryption of data for transmission over wide-area networks. The concern in DIS operations is that each human or computer participating in a simulation should not be able to acquire classified information used in the simulation without proper authorization. In DIS, multilevel security is the preferred operating mode. For example, a participating U.S. forces tank driver usually does not need and is not authorized to obtain all the information used by a participating U.S. forces intelligence analyst, and the simulator used by a participating Luftwaffe (German Air Force) fighter pilot does not need and generally is not authorized to obtain all the information that might be generated by a participating U.S. forces fighter simulator. In the former case, security is enforced by a variety of techniques, including manual procedures that the Department of Defense would like to automate. In the latter case, much of the problem is intrinsic and not amenable to automation. If a foreign pilot is not authorized to know the dash speed of a U.S. fighter at full military power, it should not be flown at that speed within range of his radar, either in a live exercise or in simulation.[51]

According to the DIS Steering Committee, the end-to-end encryption systems presently used to provide security for the communication links used by DIS are imposing severe limits on the amount of data that can be put through them.[52] The challenge is to minimize the impact of these constraints by improving the performance of the encryption systems or finding alternatives that provide adequate levels of protection but with greater throughput. The challenges and opportunities of multilevel security arise in many applications and are by no means unique to combat simulation.

2

Visual Interactivity Standards: Making It Look Real

Making it look real is at the heart of gaining acceptability for DIS and the High Level Architecture. Dr. James Jacob at Wright State University verbalized this angst: "Reality is limited by your ability to perceive it. . . . Perception is reality."[53] As such, the graphic visualization of DIS merits its own separate discussion, and perhaps even its own set of standards. The display of a DIS simulation is usually the only thing ever seen—literally—by most observers and users of a DIS synthetic environment. When you look out the canopy of an aircraft simulator, or through the view slits of a tank simulator, or out the portals of a ship simulator, or stand on the virtual deck of an aircraft carrier simulation, or ride on a "stealth observer" magic carpet through the simulated world, you are perceiving the simulated world through the manipulations of computer graphics. Yet this important interface with the human participant remains by far the weakest element in DIS.

The weakness of visualization in DIS is due to a variety of technical reasons, not a lack of desire to recreate the real world as realistically as possible. Visualization requires enormous computational capability. Historically, and until very recently, only multimillion-dollar government simulators could afford computers powerful enough to generate "out-the-window" views of the world. As a result, when technical and cost compromises were made in creating simulations, they were invariably made first in the graphics display techniques.

In the early days of SIMNET, the compromise in graphics was given a name and treated as a positive attribute, with its proponents extolling it as part of "the 60 percent solution." The implication was that attaining 60 percent of reality was a high enough level of fidelity to cause most simulation participants to become sufficiently immersed in the simulation experience to ignore the discrepancies of the missing 40 percent. Typically, this was manifested by surrounding the participant with a less than fully equipped environment; for example, a tank's crew compartment might have only a few real switches, and the rest would be painted as symbols. In the graphics realm, the

SIMNET 60 percent fidelity was typified by cartoonish graphics, with little detail in the terrain, and limitations on how far away the scenery disappeared from view.

A factor detracting from the early success of SIMNET was the low acceptability of its visual scene to the broad range of service audiences. In particular, aircrews tended to regard the mottled, cartoonish terrain texture as negative training. More recently, technological advances in computer image generation have encouraged a reevaluation of that discontent. The Air Force is pursuing technology to improve training device effectiveness, with upgrades to visual systems, sensor and radar simulation, and out-the-window scenes. Geospecific data within the visual, sensor, and radar databases will be fully correlated to ensure positive, realistic training. Images that the aircrews view on any of the navigation, targeting, radar ground map, or visual scenes will appear at the same exact geospecific location on each display, just as they would on a real-world mission.[54]

One of the first attempts to master this correlation quagmire was the integration of a DARPA-developed World Reference Model into the DARPA F-15E Weapons and Tactics Trainer. The desire for Visual Interactivity Standards (VIS), described later, is an attempt to clarify why this issue is relevant, and to propose what the simulation community can do about it. Until now, the trend has been to present the viewer with an abstraction of reality determined solely by the hardware it is viewed on. The lack of consistency among different viewers has been addressed, but it has not been possible to create an image of infinite detail and complexity akin to a high-resolution photograph, because of both hardware and software limitations.

An overriding concern of some of the most skeptical simulation users is continuing disappointing results in attempts to use advanced simulation technology to provide a visual environment that appears real to aircrews. These images are intended to be used in tactical simulations aimed at increasing mission situational awareness, assisting in mission planning and rehearsal, and improving training. At a minimum, most aircrews insist on the use of high-fidelity satellite imagery and terrain elevation data to create and display visual images matching their visual perception capabilities, at rates consistent with the dynamics of high-performance military aircraft.[55] The visual environment must be robust enough to be presented on a monitor or via a helmet-mounted device while allowing the aircrews to fly through the visual presentation in real time, either dynamically via stick and throttles or using a preprogrammed route. The terrain must appear three dimensional, with sufficient ground detail (to one square-meter resolution or better) to fly visual low-level operations. Refresh rates—the number of times per second that the visual scene is updated on the screen—must be high enough to prevent the scene from jumping or stepping as pilots pull maneuvers close to the ground, perhaps needing rates as high as fifty to sixty hertz.[56] Until recently, hardware, software, and database design issues have made satisfying these desires impractical, if not impossible.

WORLD REFERENCE MODEL

As a critical step in confronting visualization issues and thus defining Visual Interactivity Standards, DARPA set about in 1993 to define the World Reference Model (WRM).[57] DARPA recognized the limitations of a SIMNET-style graphic representation of the world and sought a generic, technology-independent method for future visualizations. The WRM was envisioned not as a hardware and software solution but as an architecture for defining the databases necessary to support a DIS synthetic environment—a virtual battlespace composed of virtual, constructive, and live simulations wired together by a DIS network. Since each DIS simulation is responsible for contributing its own component models (entities) and for presenting its users with a view (visualization) into the synthetic environment, VIS would define the relationships among these elements. The key is that VIS-defined views are customized to satisfy the operational objectives of particular simulators. The validity of the synthetic environment is dependent on the correlation of all the views within the design objectives of a DIS exercise. Achieving correlation among the out-the-window views of all the simulators requires that the objectives of the simulation be clearly defined so that a synthetic world can be created to supply each simulator with the appropriate databases. The WRM architecture defines a layered database organization supporting all the visualization data necessary to represent the required abstractions of the real world. The WRM is a framework within which simulation designers can address all the data needs to create synthetic environments.

On the surface, the WRM and a VIS approach seem rather esoteric and academic. Yet in practice, the alternative to a VIS approach can have disastrous effects on simulations. The discontinuities for non-VIS approaches can be as complex as issues of computer numerical resolution (number of data-bits); issues of terrain data source material used to draw maps; issues of common frames of reference, coordinate systems, and data conversion techniques; and issues of common databases. Take the simplest case of two simulators, a "howitzer" and a "tank," with different visualization databases. Both are modeling their own approximation of the "real world," which has rocks and trees. The graphics system for the tank shows only a relatively flat, forested terrain. The howitzer graphics system shows rocky terrain but cannot show trees. Looking "out their portals" at each other, participants in the two simulators perceive significantly different views of the world, as shown in Figure 7. The tank hides behind trees (from his perspective). The howitzer hides behind rocks (from his perspective). Neither is aware that the other's visualization is missing the crucial element (rocks or trees). The outcome of any engagement between them would be seriously skewed by their faulty perceptions of the real world.

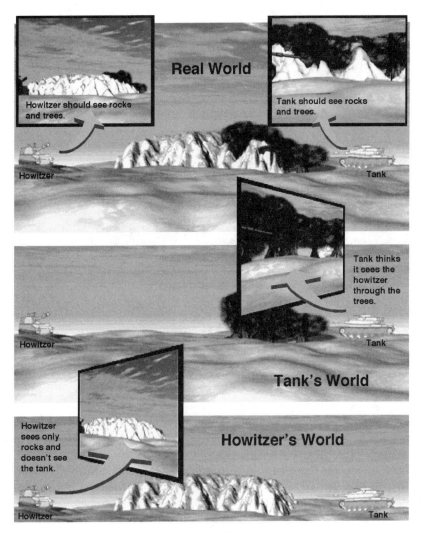

Figure 7. Scene Correlation Issues

SIMULATION COORDINATE SYSTEMS

Before discussing VIS and the WRM and assessing its applicability in alleviating visualization limitations, it is necessary to discuss coordinate systems and how they work in graphic representations. Locations in the simulated world are identified using a right-handed geocentric Cartesian coordinate system called the world coordinate system. The shape of the world is described by the world geodetic system–84 (WGS–84) standard.[58] As shown in Figure 8, the origin of the coordinate system is the centroid of the earth. The axes of this system

Figure 8. Geocentric Cartesian Coordinates

are labeled X, Y, and Z, with the positive X-axis passing through the prime meridian at the equator, the positive Y-axis passing through ninety degrees east longitude at the equator, and the positive Z-axis passing through the North Pole. These coordinates represent meters from the centroid of the earth. A sixty-four-bit double-precision floating point number represents the location for each coordinate. A distance of one unit measured in world coordinates corresponds to a distance of one meter in the simulated world, and a straight line in the world coordinate system is a straight line in the simulated world.

To describe the location and orientation of any particular entity, an entity coordinate system is associated with the entity. This is also a right-handed Cartesian coordinate system, with the distance of one unit corresponding to one meter, as in the world coordinate system. The origin of the entity coordinate system is the center of the entity's bounding volume, excluding its articulated and attached parts. The axes are labeled x, y, and z, with the positive x-axis pointing to the front of the entity, the positive y-axis pointing to the right side of the entity, and the positive z-axis pointing down out the bottom of the entity. The location of other entities can be expressed in terms of x, y, and z measured from the entities' own coordinate systems' as shown in Figure 9.

The location of an entity in relation to the rest of the simulated world is specified as the position of the origin of its entity coordinate system, expressed in world coordinates. The entity's orientation is specified using three angles that describe the successive rotations needed to transform from the world coordinate system to the entity coordinate system. These angles are called Euler angles, and they specify a set of three successive rotations about three different orthogonal axes, as depicted in Figure 10. The order of rotation is as follows: first, rotate about z by the angle Ψ (psi), then about the new y (y') by angle Θ (theta), then about the newest x (x'') by the angle Φ (phi). The positive direction of rotation about an axis is defined as clockwise when viewed toward the positive direction along the axis of rotation. The final coordinate axes are represented by x''', y''', and z'''.

TERRAIN ISSUES

Keeping in mind the definition of coordinate systems, the next topic is terrain data. The formal process of acquiring, formatting, storing, and distributing global terrain (and, more generally, environmental) data for the creation of out-the-window views is a technical policy issue that is still unresolved today. A difficult part of the process is finding a way to rapidly combine global terrain data with other data (e.g., technical intelligence on enemy weapon system platforms) to create a virtual environment for a simulation. Recognizing this, in 1995, the Defense Mapping Agency stepped up to accommodate simulation and the needs of simulators, establishing the Terrain Mapping Program Office under the auspices of the Defense Modeling and Simulation Office as the Executive Agent for Terrain.[59] In October 1996, this function was absorbed into the National

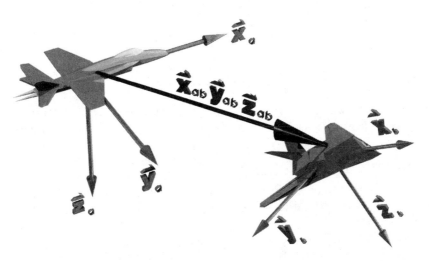

Figure 9. Entity Coordinate Systems

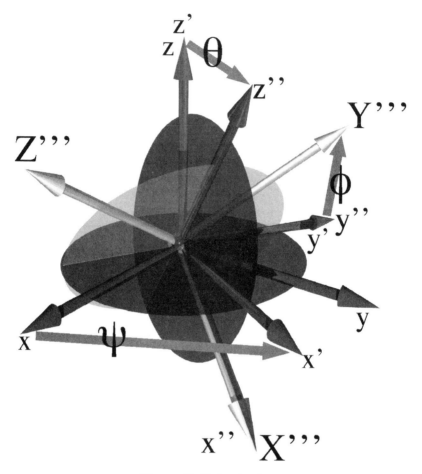

Figure 10. Euler Angles

Imagery and Mapping Agency.[60] A particularly challenging aspect is the need to model realistic changes in terrain and structures (buildings, bridges, and so forth) that would be caused by the combat activities being simulated—for example, small-arms fire, artillery fire, and aerial bombardment. That is, eventually, "dynamic terrain" must be simulated and accessible in a timely fashion.

From the first days of high-fidelity simulators with out-the-window views, real-time image-generation technology has focused on flight simulators, where the central issues were the reduction of transport delay manifested as visual lag, the improvement of frame rate to obviate jittery images, and the accurate rendering of enemy aircraft for user perceptual acceptability. With the advent of

SIMNET and the proliferation of low-cost ground-based simulation for functions such as armor and infantry, reasonable terrain imaging became vital.

Ground warfare involves extensive interaction with and modification of the terrain, including events such as tread marks and vegetation damage; cratering from bombs, artillery rounds, and mines; repairs to bridges, cratered roads, and runways; site modification and construction of berms and antitank ditches for defensive and offensive operations; and the weather effects of mud, ice, erosion, and flooding. Each of these activities and actions changes the visual character of terrain. The ability to use computer-generated visual effects to view changes in the earth's surface and properties is referred to as dynamic terrain.

In general, databases of sufficient complexity or flexibility, and image generators capable of producing numerous arbitrary modifications to the simulated terrain surface, have been beyond the realm of practicality. For certain one-of-a-kind demonstrations, ad hoc methods have been used to place bomb craters, ditches, revetments, and the like at specific predetermined locations within visual databases, to be called on by rote as needed during a simulation exercise. However, in any large-scale or long-duration free-play combat exercise, it is difficult to predict where each and every terrain modification would occur in order to pre-position them.

One approach to dynamic terrain uses client-server distributed computing. The client-server consists of a heterogeneous cluster of high-performance workstations and a variety of parallel and vector supercomputers. In this arrangement, a single workstation acts as the primary terrain controller. It manages the operation of all other computers involved in the terrain-generation process. This allows for maximum flexibility, permitting changes in the available computing power in response to specific terrain computational requirements. This implementation produces high-detail terrain that is responsive to rapidly changing battlefield conditions in a real-time environment. This enhances the realism of combat simulations.[61] However, to facilitate this, a standard creation and correlation scheme must be adopted among all users. This scheme is the intent of VIS and the WRM.

VIS AND THE WRM PROCESS

Paraphrasing Brockway's discussion of the World Reference Model,[62] the WRM is "grounded" on the premise that advanced distributed simulations will be truly heterogeneous and completely dynamic. The point of the WRM is to satisfy the need for a simulator-independent approach to producing visualization data. At the center of the WRM is the synthetic world. It characterizes the data used to make simulator databases and addresses the types of operations that must be performed to massage the data for simulation use. Traditionally, each creator of a simulator designed and manufactured its own version of the data, data storage, and data access for its simulator visualization system. The result has been that every out-the-window view of the same scene looks significantly different. It is the goal of the synthetic world to draw on the similarities among the many redundant simulation database production processes and build in consistency.

The WRM is intended to provide a framework for:

• The flow of source data into simulator databases

• The provision of intermediate products to share data at various points along the refinement path

   • The use of consistent coordinate systems, projections, and conversions

   • The application of standard attributes among types of data

• The specification of simulation and simulator requirements that affect the format of the data

   • Consideration of the issues associated with dynamic terrain

When laid out as the flowchart in Figure 11, the World Reference Model consists of the building-block elements of the real world, the maps, the synthetic world, the simulator databases, and the synthetic environments consisting of live, virtual, and constructive simulations connected by a DIS network.

In the WRM, the real world is the physical geographic area to be simulated. It is unconstrained in size and might be as small as a road intersection or the inside of a building or as large as the entire globe.

The maps for the WRM can be derived from any data source. They might be derived from a paper product, a digital elevation or cultural database, or an imagery system or product. The maps represent measurements and data collected from the real world. They are often conveyed in "thematic layers,"

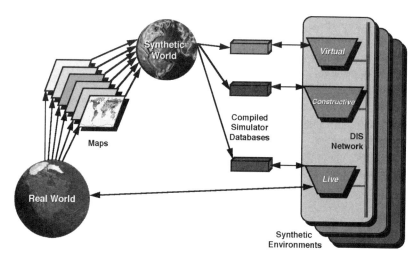

Figure 11. World Reference Model Flowchart

where measurements of one type are stored together without relationship to any other type of measurement. For example, the National Imagery and Mapping Agency's Digital Terrain Elevation Data (height of the terrain) and Digital Feature Attribute Data (buildings, roads, and so forth) are stored separately, in different formats, even though they may cover the same geographic area. These separate layers of data cause problems for developers of visualization systems, because the interrelationships among the data may be lost. For example, the shape and location of a lake depend on the surrounding terrain, not just a feature on a map labeled "lake." If the terrain data do not match the shape of the lake, in a visualization, the water could appear to climb uphill.

The WRM synthetic world is the focus of the VIS process. It is at this point that the map source data coalesce into a single integrated database that defines the spatial context of the synthetic environment. The synthetic world is where the thematic layers are reintegrated and consistency conflicts are resolved. The unified spatial data of the synthetic world define the ground truth for VIS. Table 4 describes the essentials for building a synthetic world database.

The crowning step in VIS is to prepare the individual simulator databases from the WRM and apply them in the synthetic environments. The simulator databases are extractions of data from the synthetic world, formatted to the application and performance criteria of specific simulators. It is at this point, and not before, that optimization for hardware and software specifics is accounted for, addressing such visualization issues as polygon mesh generation, effect of materials on color and textures, and levels of detail.

Finally, the WRM products are used in the synthetic environments to satisfy particular live, virtual, and constructive simulation requirements. A synthetic environment is composed of those simulators that can present the appropriate VIS views of the synthetic world. The intent is for many synthetic environments to be extracted from a single synthetic world, dependent only on the specific requirements of the simulators engaged in that particular simulation activity.

In implementation, the WRM methodology of applying VIS includes these steps:

• Identify the scope of the synthetic environment. Define user objectives, geographic area, and terrain requirements.

• Identify the simulations to be supported. Include simulators that are likely to be supported in the future.

• Identify the database products required to support the simulations.

• Analyze the thematic layers needed to support all the simulators.

• Search for mapping products and existing digital databases.

• Design the synthetic environment. Balance the goals, technology, data availability, risk, time, and money.

• Produce a master design document describing the synthetic environment. Include the correlation metrics against which all views will be measured.

TABLE 4: DATABASE ESSENTIALS

- Select appropriate input sources.
- Evaluate the relationships among existing thematic layers in the layered data models.
- Resolve the attributes of how the sources of data are encoded (e.g., different ground materials, cultural features, terrain features).
- Resolve the coordinate systems so that all data are referenced to a single datum, with preference given to WGS–84 for compatibility with the National Imagery and Mapping Agency's digital world.
- Resolve the intralayer topology (e.g., how the elements, such as road networks, railroads, power lines, and rivers, are interrelated and connected).
- Resolve the interlayer topology (e.g., a valley in Digital Terrain Elevation Data as related to a river in Digital Feature Attribute Data).
- Resolve the effects of data generalization, such as the smoothing out of terrain features, rivers, and so forth.
- Create a consistent process for layered to spatial conversion of the products.
- Produce a spatial data model that assimilates the topology and topography for the simulation but can be compiled, as required, for varying simulator optimization schemes.
- Collaborate on three-dimensional modeling specifications so that the product visualizations will adhere to correlation metrics.
- Mechanize the database export process for the distribution of specific simulator optimized visualization products.

- Design the synthetic world. Define a data flow that includes all the thematic layers and simulator databases, as well as all the necessary transformations.
- Test views (i.e., presentations and simulations) against correlation metrics and suitability to users' objectives.

To make it self-consistent, the data organization for the VIS world is as follows:

- Data representations (raster, vector, topologic)
- Thematic layering (terrain skin, transportation, vegetation)

- Domain layering (global, regional, local, pedestrian)
- Coordinate systems (geocentric, geographic, geodetic)
- Configuration control (naming and version numbers)
- Correlation metrics (position, color, topology, trafficability)

Adoption by the DIS community of a standardized, hardware- and software-independent visualization database process, such as the Visual Interactivity Standards World Reference Model described here, will go a long way toward resolving contemporary issues of correlation and interoperability among simulations.

3

Simulation for Training

Since the advent of computers, computer simulation has been used for training in one form or another. Of interest here is the undisputed, notable success of interactive simulation used for training. The combination of network technology and low-cost computer hardware for simulation graphics has made whole new realms of training environments possible.

SIMULATION NETWORKING—SIMNET

The SIMNET program was the first demonstration that multiple moderately priced simulators interacting via high-speed data networks could create a virtual battlespace with sufficient realism that military units could practice maneuvering, communicating, and fighting with the look and feel of an actual battle. According to Colonel Jack Thorpe, U.S. Air Force, the DARPA program manager responsible for its development, "In SIMNET, combat forces and their commanders must move, shoot, communicate and navigate just as they do in battle, with all the chaos, stress, boldness, incompetence, risk and precision of combat."[63] The requirements of the SIMNET system were to allow combined arms training with normal command chains, complete visual contact with the enemy and battlefield, mobility to close with or evade the enemy, and the ability to suppress enemy fire, destroy the enemy, and win the battle under realistic conditions of war.

The original SIMNET concept was a linkage of hundreds of armored vehicle simulators at Fort Knox, Kentucky, to a lesser number of aviation simulators at Fort Rucker, Alabama. The program was initiated in 1982 and completed in 1989. Each simulator cost approximately $200,000 and consisted of an independent fiberglass crew compartment with microprocessors, out-the-window graphics, sound, controls, instruments, and a computer-graphics terrain database. The simulators were aesthetically designed to enhance the sense of realism for the operators, but only those instruments, dials, gauges, and switches that contributed directly to combat operations were functional. SIMNET employed "selective fidelity"[64] to provide 60 percent of the real-systems capabilities, using off-the-shelf computer hardware and software to keep the cost down to one-hundredth that of a traditional high-fidelity multiaxis motion simulator. As mentioned earlier, Colonel Thorpe contended that SIMNET would "allow already highly trained soldiers to earn their Ph.D.'s in warfighting."[65]

As the forerunner of Distributed Interactive Simulation, SIMNET started with local-area networks within a single facility. Platoons of armor simulators were connected with coaxial cables. The local network was augmented by a SIMNET Mission Management, Command, and Control system that created the surrogate battlespace and other elements during exercises. At the battalion level, commanders controlled a tactical operations center, administration, and logistics, as well as other fire support, close air support, fuel and munitions supply, and mobile maintenance functions. Each staff function was simulated on an Apple Macintosh computer connected to the local-area network via Appletalk software and hardware.[66]

As mentioned earlier, the computer graphics for SIMNET were its weakest point; they were deliberately kept at a low level of fidelity to reduce cost.[67] The graphics consisted of artificially textured triangular polygons to form the terrain skin or ground, generic trees, and buildings and relatively faithfully reproduced models of vehicles. The combat arena for SIMNET was constrained by the hardware memory of the graphics computers and typically was limited to tens of square kilometers, so that at any time, each combatant was constrained within a local terrain patch of a couple of square kilometers.[68]

Alongside the original SIMNET facility at Fort Knox was the SIMNET developmental site (SIMNET-D), conceived along the line of Lockheed's famed "Skunk Works."[69] Fashioned as the prototyping complex for simulation, it was at SIMNET-D that simulators with the ability to be reconfigured were first networked and used to create and test new concepts in forward air defense, global positioning system use, communications, and laser targeting systems. SIMNET-D was transferred from DARPA to the Army in 1992.

COMBINED ARMS TACTICAL TRAINER

The Army is spending several hundred million dollars a year on simulation for training, with particular emphasis on pursuing technological advances in the areas of increased fidelity, performance measurement, and networking.[70] Perhaps the most prominent training program is the Combined Arms Tactical Trainer program. It was initiated to build on the success of the SIMNET armor and aviation training systems of the 1980s and to modernize them across the Army's mission areas. It is composed of five major components: the Aviation Combined Arms Tactical Trainer, the Air Defense Combined Arms Tactical Trainer, the Engineer Combined Arms Tactical Trainer, the Fire Support Combined Arms Tactical Trainer, and the Combined Combat Training Facility. The latter will contain the human-centered simulators to simulate the Task Force Tactical Ops Center, high-mobility multiwheeled vehicles, dismounted infantry, M2/M3 Bradley Fighting Vehicles, M1A1/A2 Abrams tanks, M-901 improved

TOW vehicles, M-113 armored personnel carriers, M-981 FIST-V/fire support team vehicles, and semiautomated forces to model other Blue and Red forces. Development was begun in 1992, with the first trainer to be delivered in 1997. A significant strength of these simulators is the visualization of atmospheric conditions, including cloud cover, haze, smoke, and ambient temperature, and the rendering of images based on precalculated radiances and parametric adjustments stored in the database for each terrain or target component. The Army's new emphasis on the visual representation of the synthetic environment breaks from the earlier 60 percent solution of SIMNET.

SYNTHETIC THEATER OF WAR

The DARPA-led Synthetic Theater of War (STOW) program is the estimated $1 billion development of a demonstration of joint operations in synthetic environments.[71] The project combines live, virtual, and constructive simulation to provide a realistic joint-task-force environment, range instrumentation, and interfaces. The program seeks to replicate up to 15,000 soldiers, tanks, or aircraft in a battlespace. It aims to encourage improvements in high-speed networking technology, computer-generated semiautomated forces, and other distributed simulation technologies.[72] STOW targets distributed simulation shortcomings, such as difficulties in cross-coupling legacy (previously existing) simulations, problems in integrating live (peopled) simulations and semi-autonomous forces in the same battlespace, low perceived realism, and lack of current operational concepts.[73] STOW includes a series of advanced concept technology demonstrations, including STOW–Europe (STOW–E) in November 1994, STOW–97, and Advanced Distributed Simulation 2000.[74]

STOW–E
- Brigade Task Force—one virtual battalion, one constructive battalion, and one live battalion with instrumented plus other combined and joint assets.
- Subset of REFORGER 94 (joint task force exercise) with a related scenario, limited connectivity.
- Limited Air Force and Navy participation.

STOW–97
- Capable of simulating up to a joint task force.
- Includes an aggressive, capable opposing force.
- Focused on training and readiness.
- Contains virtual simulation of command and control at a low level.
- Distributed with a limited dynamic—free play—environment.
- Integrates live forces from instrumented ranges in the southwestern United States.

Advanced Distributed Simulation 2000
- Appropriate functionality across a theater of war.
- Functionality to support a broad range of defense functions.
- Tactically significant dynamic environments.
- Intelligent behavior of automated forces.
- Behaviors for higher-level headquarters.
- Embedded, deployable, live instrumentation technology.

In developing STOW, DARPA recognized that simulations must accurately portray the entire joint and multinational battlespace across the spectrum of training and operational planning. This DARPA focus was strongly supported by the rest of the Department of Defense simulation community. DARPA closely coordinated the STOW effort with U.S. forces and the Joint Staff and pursued the development of a common framework for theater-level training simulations.[75] However, in 1996, STOW began to face opposition from the user community, which felt that STOW was not being developed to meet its requirements.[76] DARPA undertook an assessment of the STOW program and concluded that STOW was on track.

STOW development has been augmented by several other DARPA advanced distributed simulation initiatives. These include training simulations for battalion- and brigade-level operations, readiness simulation focusing on battle staff synchronization, small-unit collective training, combat service support, individual training, and the development of high-fidelity, low-cost distributed simulation weapons and tactics trainers, such as the operationally representative DARPA F-15E Weapons and Tactics Trainer—a fully functional, high-fidelity cockpit simulator. The STOW environment exploited the DARPA Command and Control simulation facility to provide technical and operational oversight of simulation exercises, in conjunction with the SimCore discrete event simulation framework as the exercise scenario generator, manager, and master controller.

Synthetic Theater of War–Europe
DARPA, the U.S. Army Europe and Seventh Army, and U.S. Army Simulation, Training, and Instrumentation Command together created the STOW–E project. The purpose of STOW–E was to develop a synthetic theater of war environment in Europe by linking virtual and constructive simulations with live maneuvers through the instrumentation system at the Combat Maneuver Training Center. By "expanding" the battlespace available to task force commanders conducting training exercises at Hohenfels Training Area at the European Combat Maneuver Training Center, STOW–E overcame the constricted maneuver space for live forces and improved the realism of the training environment. The "expansion" was accomplished through the linkage between SIMNET

simulators, the Brigade Battalion Battle Simulation, and the Instrumentation System at the Combat Maneuver Training Center.

STOW–E was incorporated into the Atlantic Resolve exercise in November 1994. A commanders-in-chief initiative, STOW–E was destined to create a brigade-level training environment to raise the Combat Maneuver Training Center entry-level proficiency of all tactical echelon rotations. Higher entry-level proficiency was expected to result in greater combat readiness by the end of training at the center.

STOW–E demonstrated a number of new environmental effects on a synthetic battlefield, including illumination flares, signal flares, and signal smoke; dynamic time-of-day wind effects (velocity and direction); concertina wire, battlefield smoke, and obscurants; minefield breaching; dust storm, rain, fog, and haze; preemplaced survivability positions and obstacles; and multistate objects (bridges and buildings).

It also demonstrated the following synthetic forces capabilities: five ships (maneuvering and damage); sensors and weapons functionality; eighteen new U.S. Marine Corps entity types; intelligence forces, fixed-wing aircraft engaged in defensive air, close air support, and combined strike and rotary-wing aircraft engaged in armed reconnaissance and attack; forward air controller operations; destruction of bridges that provide a barrier to ground vehicles; tanks that deploy smoke and change speed and formation when entering or leaving smoke screen; forward observer detection, classification, and reporting of targets; and a company team commander who can receive and send command and control software interface language messages and plan and replan missions.

STOW–E leveraged work completed by DARPA on the overall STOW project. The Defense Simulation Internet played a major role in supporting the communications requirements for STOW–E. The STOW–E exercise incorporated thirteen Defense Simulation Internet sites and over 3,500 entities. Participating STOW–E sites were in the continental United States, Germany, and England.

Synthetic Theater of War–97

The STOW–97 Advanced Concept Technology Demonstration was jointly sponsored by DARPA and the U. S. Atlantic Command.[77] The goal was to provide an operational demonstration of advanced distributed simulation technologies to directly support joint training and mission rehearsal. The demonstration paved the way for a common simulation environment that is usable across the spectrum of service and joint training, crisis rehearsal, doctrine development, battle planning, resource readiness assessment, material development, and system acquisition.

Critical technologies relevant to STOW–97 created a synthetic battlespace consisting of high-resolution terrain, tactically significant environmental effects, behaviorally accurate computer-generated forces and command and control entities, and a simulation infrastructure compliant with the Department of Defense High Level Architecture. The synthetic theater of war simulations are distributed over a global network using the latest asynchronous transfer mode and multicast technologies.

Early in Fiscal Year 1996, it was decided that STOW–97 would become a prototype federation for the High Level Architecture. This decision placed new requirements on the STOW program to reengineer synthetic environments and synthetic forces software to comply with the High Level Architecture object-oriented framework. It also required the development of a Runtime Infra-structure that would act as a standard data transport mechanism for all future Department of Defense simulations.

STOW–97 includes a cooperative research and development agreement between the United States and the United Kingdom. Under this agreement, the two countries are working toward the development of international standards for modeling and simulation in accordance with the High Level Architecture initiative.

EAST COAST LITTORAL WARFARE TRAINING COMPLEX

Within the Department of Defense, considerable emphasis is being placed on creating a suitable joint training battlespace and each of the Services is con-tending to pull it together. According to Vince Grimes,[78] the Navy's desire to participate is embodied in the initiative for an East Coast Littoral Warfare Training Complex. This environment includes Navy, Coast Guard, Marine, Army, and Air Force training ranges along the East Coast between Norfolk and Langley, Virginia, and Camp Lejeune, North Carolina. The complex will enable the Services to conduct command, control, communications, and intelligence training and perform complicated air, land, and sea force-on-force threat envi-ronment exercises with live and virtual weapon systems connected into a virtual combat environment. It will include secure data links and encryption, non-intrusive data collection, improved semiautomated forces, and tactical environ-ment simulation, as well as sophisticated electronic assessment and debriefing systems. The architects for the new environment are determined to capitalize on the capabilities evidenced in DIS.

TRAINING FOR BOSNIA AND KOREA

In the spring of 1993, DARPA was tasked by the U.S. Army to build a three-dimensional visualization database of Bosnia for training U.S. forces. The sys-tem was created by the Army Topographic Engineering Center and received rave reviews from Army staff and operational personnel. It provided a quick-look opportunity for personnel to drive and fly their vehicles through the tor-tuous valleys, canyons, and mountain roads of Bosnia. This enabled military planners to grasp the significance of the severe terrain and the vulnerability of ground forces on the narrow choke points of the roadways.

The three-dimensional visualization of Bosnia was put to the test in 1995 by U.S. forces planning and executing Operation Deliberate Force. The Defense Mapping Agency applied a commercial variant of the technology to enable pilots to "fly through" and visualize their targets before they flew their missions. The three-dimensional visualization was so successful that after a matter of days, "No pilot took off without first using the system to rehearse the mission."[79]

A similar database and three-dimensional visualization system were used in support of the Balkan peace negotiations in November 1995 in Dayton, Ohio. As the peace negotiators and delegates refined geographic requirements to peaceful resolution of the conflict, three-dimensional displays of the terrain were projected using Defense Mapping Agency digital imagery and Digital Terrain Elevation Data.

Similar databases have been created for other locations, such as Korea. These visualization databases are the first essential step in creating a synthetic environment that can be used in distributed simulation to investigate the implications of a new operational domain.

BATTLESPACE VISUALIZATION FOR VIRTUAL DOMINANCE

Within the Army, the Deputy Chief of Staff for Operations and Plans (DCSOPS) has assumed responsibility for the task of battlefield visualization. DCSOPS and the Army Training and Doctrine Command are refining the new doctrine and introducing the notion of the battlespace, "the use of the entire battlefield and the space around it to apply combat power to overwhelm the enemy."[80] The concept includes not only the physical volume of breadth, depth, and height but also the operational dimensions of time, tempo, depth, and synchronization. "Commanders must dominate the enemy battlespace through a comprehensive understanding of geography and terrain, available collection assets and available weapon systems."[81]

The desire for battlespace dominance leads to the requirement for battlespace visualization. The ability to see the relationships among enemy forces, friendly forces, the environment, and the desired end state is akin to virtual dominance. A clear and complete image of the commander's entire battlespace is critical to effective mission accomplishment, because it drives the entire mission planning and execution processes. The technology of DIS enables the commander to envisage the battlespace dynamically, seeing the flow of operations and activities from start to finish. DIS for training has come a long way from the initial SIMNET system.

4

Simulation for Acquisition

Like entropy—always expanding—the systems engineering process in acquisition has become more complex, expensive, and time-consuming. With the continued high visibility of the shredded defense budget in both the congressional and the private sectors, and the true nature of any long-term reforms of the acquisition process undetermined, the need to improve and expedite the systems engineering process in favor of quality end items has never been greater. As represented in Figure 12, a typical program commits 70 to 90 percent of its life-cycle funds to a critical path in the first 10 to 30 percent of the program's scheduled time.

From the time a new weapon system concept is conceived until the systems engineering process is at the implementation of life-cycle support stage, ten to fourteen years have normally passed. At the 70 to 90 percent stage of system development, when 10 to 15 percent of the funds are still available as "unobligated," requirements are still being fine-tuned at the detail level, and their validity is frequently being questioned at the macro level. It is in the refinement of system requirements that simulation can provide significant cost savings and added value.

MIL-STD 499B defines systems engineering "as an interdisciplinary approach to evolve and verify an integrated and optimally balanced set of product and process designs that satisfy user needs and provide information for management decision making." The standard describes the systems engineering process as a "comprehensive, iterative process that transforms identified objectives into a set of life-cycle optimized product and process descriptions that satisfy those objectives. The systems engineering process includes requirements analysis, functional analysis and allocation, synthesis, and system analysis and control." The principal idea herein is that the use of DIS synthetic environments provides an extraordinary tool to effectively and efficiently assist in the systems engineering process and to move its impact to the front end of a program.

In August 1995, Dr. Pat Sanders, Director of the Office of Test, System Engineering and Evaluation, commissioned a one-year study with the objective of assessing the effectiveness of the use of modeling and simulation in the acquisition process. Specifically, she was "looking for metrics by which the

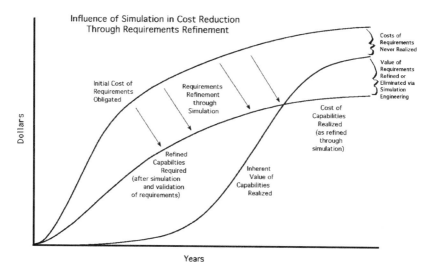

Figure 12. Commitment of Funds

Department of Defense could ascertain the value—if any—that was returned on its investment in modeling and simulation in terms of reduction in time, resources and risk in weapons system development and fielding in terms of increase in the military utility of those systems."[82] The report, published in October 1996, attests to tangible, quantitative indicators that the use of modeling and simulation can provide substantial benefits measured in time, cost, productivity, and system quality and performance.

As perhaps the progenitor of the idea to use DIS as a systems engineering tool for acquisition, DARPA has, since 1990, aggressively pursued interoperable simulation as a highly leveragable technology to significantly enhance the systems engineering process.[83] One of the problems associated with the process of systems engineering for large new weapon systems has always been the traditional linear fashion of the engineering approach.[84] DARPA hoped to create a new methodology using simulation that would directly involve the customers with the developers of a product. Using distributed simulation via local- and wide-area networks, DARPA thought that the new simulation tool-set would support a streamlining of the systems engineering processes. Through a variety of interwoven technology programs, DARPA set out to create a virtual battlespace in which government and industry could work together. Four of these virtual battlespace programs were the Synthetic Environment for Requirements and Concepts Evaluation and Synthesis (SERCES) program, the Zealous Pursuit program, the Zen Regard program, and the Simulation-Based Design program. SERCES was to pursue non-DARPA acquisition program issues, Zealous Pursuit was to investigate the feasibility of creating a systems engineering environment, Zen Regard was to build a systems engineering environment for a complex DARPA technology demonstration program, and Simulation-Based Design was to create a distributed, collaborative virtual development environment.

SERCES

DARPA Director Victor Reis advocated the SERCES program.[85] It was initiated in January 1991 as a collaboration between DARPA and the Joint Program Office for Unmanned Air Vehicles. DARPA wanted to experiment with the application of DIS to the entire acquisition life cycle of an actual Department of Defense program, from pre–milestone 0 through development, production, employment, operations, and support.

Under the SERCES program, DARPA sought to create a model for a future systems engineering process. This model tied together an engineering and manufacturing knowledge base from commercial industry and an acquisition and operations knowledge base possessed by the government. The aim of SERCES was to involve the end-item system operational users, military personnel, civilian government personnel, commercial industry personnel, and potential end-item system and subsystem manufacturers and logistics support agents in the systems engineering process.

The Navy proposed the Maritime Unmanned Air Vehicle to DARPA as a candidate program. The SERCES program was tailored to fit the specific simulation requirements of the Navy program, while attempting to retain generic applicability. The combined effort was pursued through one full simulation cycle, wherein significant operational findings were discovered. SERCES took the first steps to examine closely the application of advanced technologies in simulation and local and long-haul networking of distributed simulations to support and improve the systems engineering process. In that regard, SERCES included a case study of the Navy's Maritime Unmanned Aerial Vehicle.[86] One of the successful outgrowths of the program was a hierarchical process model describing in software the functional flow of information and the decision-making process for the Joint Program Office. In 1993, the Navy formally canceled the Maritime Unmanned Air Vehicle program, and the remaining DARPA SERCES effort was used to support other programs.[87]

ZEALOUS PURSUIT

Following the end of Desert Storm in the winter of 1991, Reis tasked DARPA to explore technologies that could enhance U.S. forces' ability to perform missions that had not been successfully completed in the Gulf War. One prominent deficiency was the inability to find and destroy mobile missiles. These targets were significant not because of their military effectiveness but because of the sociopolitical ramifications of the enemy holding noncombatant populations at risk.

At Reis's behest, DARPA initiated research to "master the information flow" in warfighting,[88] initially based on the problem of finding mobile missile targets. The diverse and disparate nature of the individual elements of the problem—crossing all bounds across all Services and other agencies, and spanning intelligence collection, data fusion, information distribution, operational employment, and target execution—lent it to unique architectural evaluation techniques. DARPA's Colonel Jack Thorpe convinced Reis to attempt to exploit the potential strength of DIS as a method to visualize, qualitatively evaluate, and perhaps quantify technological components and tactical concepts before investing in operational hardware and software for finding mobile missiles.

Following Thorpe's vision, in 1992, DARPA put together a secure simulation system connecting seven sites around the United States. The interactive simulation included manned simulators for over twenty types of weapon systems, including aircraft, satellites, intelligence collection systems, theater ballistic missiles, tanks, and unmanned air vehicles. The simulation system was built with SIMNET technology. Thirty-seven Army, Navy, Air Force, other government agency, and contractor organizations participated in the construction and conduct of the simulations. Simulation exercises were run in October, November, and December 1992, with a scenario based on a twelve-hour period during Desert Storm. In addition, twenty short simulations were run in December 1992 for 568 senior Department of Defense visitors to observe. The exercises provided limited operational insight into the mission difficulties of finding mobile missiles, but they did provide significant lessons about the building of large-scale distributed simulations across multiple organizations.[89]

ZEN REGARD
Following the technical engineering success of Zealous Pursuit, DARPA reengineered the SIMNET-based distributed simulation environment in 1993 and created the single most complex and robust DIS secure interactive warfighting simulation to that date, known as Zen Regard. With Zen Regard, DARPA took a unique approach to the use of distributed simulation. DARPA wanted (1) a robust theater of war for the insertion of technology concepts and (2) direct participation by the services in the evaluation of operational concepts. The Army, Navy, and Air Force were invited to define and orchestrate the simulation environment for Zen Regard. The Services formulated the simulation scenarios, the C4I architecture, the order of battle for Red and Blue forces, and the rules of engagement for mission execution. Then DARPA built the distributed simulation environment (see Figure 13) and planned the exercises. The actual simulation exercises of Zen Regard were populated by operational personnel from the Army, Navy, and Air Force.[90]

With the intent of conducting systems engineering in Zen Regard, DARPA began creating a unique distributed simulation facility to house the technical

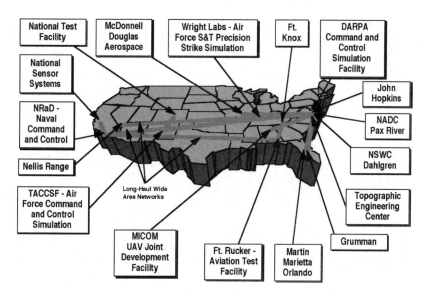

Figure 13. Zen Regard Simulation Sites

development teams as well as the operational simulation participants. What evolved was a prototypical stage for masterminding and executing large-scale distributed simulation exercises. Referred to simply as the Command and Control simulation facility, it was deliberately fashioned by Herman Zimmerman to transcend parochial views of command and control and place users in a future-oriented frame of reference.[91] The secure facility in Arlington, Virginia, was the centerpiece of a wide-area network linking the Zen Regard simulation sites. The facility was equipped with a vast array of state-of-the-art graphics computers, secure video teleconferencing, and simulation infrastructure. The theatrical-sized video wall displays (see Figure 14) presented operators with three-dimensional out-the-window views of the battlespace. Map table video displays (see Figure 15) provided more traditional two-dimensional electronic "paper" maps. In a command and control role, the facility provided operators with situational awareness previously unrealized through the multimedia fusion of intelligence and warfighting data with advanced graphics.

The facility was used daily as the software development and test and evaluation site for Zen Regard (see Figure 16), and during Zen Regard exercises, it was the hub for joint command and control.

The facility was connected to other facilities at multiple levels of security, enabling it to act as the intelligence focal point for exercise operations. The concepts prototyped in the Command and Control simulation facility were precursors to programs such as the Air Force's Virtual Reality Command and

Figure 14. Command Console: DARPA Command and Control Simulation Facility

Figure 15. Operations Pod: DARPA Command and Control Simulation Facility

Control System.[92] In 1996, DARPA successfully transferred the Command and Control Simulation facility to an end user, the Army Missile Command in Huntsville, Alabama.

Zen Regard and its associated exercises exemplified the development and use of DIS as a tool for a complex acquisition program. It eventually reached over twenty sites around the United States, connected by secure wide-area high-

Figure 16. Engineering Pod: DARPA Command and Control Simulation Facility

speed networks of various types. It encompassed the operational and tactical representation of almost every aspect of theater warfare, including national technical means intelligence collection, processes, and products; Tomahawk land attack missiles launched from submarines; Apache helicopter suppression of enemy air defense; a joint surveillance and target attack radar system; F-15Es dropping laser-guided bombs; and M1A1 tanks attacking enemy armor.

In addressing one of the long-term challenges in gaining acceptance for DIS, Zen Regard and its antecedents attempted to determine whether DIS synthetic environments could be linked with real-world live simulation. Skeptics viewed the integration of DIS and the highly dynamic action of fighter aircraft on a live range as a tremendously difficult if not impossible task. In 1993, DARPA set out to solve that problem. Using the PDUs of DIS version 2.0.3, DARPA and the Air Force Institute of Technology developed an interface with the Nellis Test Range Red Flag Measurement and Debriefing System (RFMDS) that was compliant with DIS standards. Experiments using this interface were conducted during February 1994. The object of the experiments was to show that the DIS protocols could be used effectively to transmit aircraft telemetry to remote sites in real time for the training and debriefing of aircrews, ultimately allowing the integration of live and virtual simulations. As a final test of this phase of the project, the Nellis Range RFMDS was connected to the DARPA Command and Control simulation facility in Arlington using a standard telecommunications T-1 line.

The Nellis Range is approximately 12,000 square miles of land north of Las Vegas, Nevada, that is predominantly open desert, with a few scattered mountains and an occasional ranch. The range is used to teach maneuvers in mock aerial battles that will prepare aircrews for real battles. The aircraft instrumentation subsystem collects environmental information along with information from the aircraft's instruments, which is then relayed to the ground tracking units. On the ground, the tracking instrumentation subsystem captures the information for as many as thirty-six high-activity aircraft. In addition, ground tracking radar units are used to track as many as 100 low-activity aircraft. All this information is combined and relayed to Nellis Air Force Base by a combination of fiber-optic connections and microwave transmitters. At Nellis, the data are processed in real time in a Perkin Elmer mainframe computer used as the control and computation subsystem. After the data are processed, they are passed to various systems, including the display and debriefing subsystem consoles and a computer for map generation. The connection to the RFMDS for this experiment was in a listen-only mode to prevent any interference with the training exercise.

During this experiment, and while actual live exercises were ongoing at the Nellis Range, the telemetry data from the thirty-six live-range aircraft were converted to DIS PDUs, sent across the wide-area network to the DARPA Command and Control simulation facility in Arlington, and then displayed in the form of two- and three-dimensional icons on situational displays. In addition, live-range video and live tactical radio voice circuits were transmitted across the network to Arlington. This real-time data transfer provided an unparalleled situational awareness of the ongoing exercise and was the first big step toward the integration of live and virtual simulation.

Another step in linking the live and virtual simulation worlds is the creation of low-cost, high-fidelity cockpit simulators capable of operating on a DIS network. This implies a new generation of unit-level training devices that can be used by flying squadrons in conjunction with the integration of live simulation. These can even replace expensive-to-maintain operational flight trainer simulators. The new devices will consist of high-fidelity cockpit mock-ups and pilot-friendly instructor-operator stations integrated into the DIS environment. The hardware will be based on the latest commercial off-the-shelf computer processor technology, while the software will be functionally identical to the actual aircraft avionics operational flight programs.[93]

One of these built-for-DIS simulations is the DARPA-funded F-15E Weapons and Tactics Trainer (see Figure 17).[94] It was originally conceived to go beyond the 60 percent simulator solution of the SIMNET era, concentrating on maximizing user acceptance of the simulation device while minimizing production costs. In the process, it was designed to be fully DIS integrated, so that it could literally be taken and set up anywhere, be plugged into a network, and participate in a DIS virtual battlespace. The DARPA F-15E simulator broke new ground on the myriad technical requirements of interaction among visual, electromagnetic, navigation, and physical terrain databases and forged a new understanding of the difficult issue of perceiving and reacting to tens of thousands of other simulation entities in a virtual battlespace. Its total cost, including non-

Figure 17. DARPA F-15E Weapons and Tactics Trainer

recurring research and development costs, was less than one year of the operations and maintenance budget for an equivalent high-fidelity F-15E dome simulator, and less than one-twentieth of the procurement cost for a new high-fidelity F-15E dome simulator. When DARPA completed its simulator development, the product was well received by the Air Force operational community. The reaction was such a turnabout that ongoing Air Force acquisition plans were modified to procure additional units of the DARPA F-15E instead of a competing non-DIS simulator.

Beyond the technical feats of Zen Regard in conducting live and virtual DIS exercises and developing new generations of simulators, there was a significant outcome in operations. In an effort such as Zen Regard, there was the clear need for defined and understood joint roles and responsibilities among the participants, as well as among all the participating organizations (Department of Defense and Industry). The heat of battle, even simulated, is less than an optimal time to discuss who's on first. But with a DIS synthetic environment such as Zen Regard, there was the flexibility to try new operational concepts in a controllable but completely free-play battlespace. Zen Regard opened new vistas on how joint warfighting issues of command and control could be visualized. It laid the groundwork for defining a new generation of simulation architectures.

SIMULATION-BASED DESIGN
Simulation-Based Design integrates the technologies of distributed simulation, physics-based modeling, and virtual environments to perform virtual prototyping

in a synthetic environment.[95] The Simulation-Based Design program utilizes high-data-rate networks to integrate program resources (people, systems, and data) distributed across the United States. The program provides digital mockups through advanced visualization methods to accurately simulate the total physical system and its operation. In the October 1996 report on the use of simulation for acquisition, the Simulation-Based Design program was lauded as one of the key efforts to "revolutionize the Acquisition Process for complex military and commercial products."[96] The Simulation-Based Design program:

• Permits detailed evaluation of product and process designs early in the life cycle, reducing expensive surprises later during manufacturing and operational service.

• Eliminates costly prototypes for both product and process designs.

• Provides realistic operator interaction with the product during the requirement and design process.

• Permits the development of tactics and training in realistic operational scenarios with existing operational assets.

The overall technical approach for the Simulation-Based Design program separates it into three components: core architecture development and demonstration, enabling technology development, and system utility demonstration projects. The primary focus of the program is the core architecture development. Both enabling technology development and system utility demonstrations serve to improve and build on the core architecture. The core architecture includes high-performance networking services, user interfaces and tools, methodologies and supporting software for distributed collaboration, and intelligent, distributed database structures. Although no specific product was intended to be designed or developed, initially, a generic surface combatant ship was chosen as the object of product development.

The early phases of the program consisted of small-scale demonstrations applied to ship design to determine the program's potential and identify critical areas of development. To successfully implement simulation, integrated product and process development, and virtual prototyping, the Simulation-Based Design program had to:

• Visualize and interact with large, complex geometry, on the order of thirty million objects and one million polygons, updated thirty times per second.

• Generate, calculate, and evaluate more than 1,000 designs with hundreds of parameters.

• Seamlessly alter fidelity in both geometry and feature space.

• Maintain and verify completeness of systems using databases requiring more than 200 gigabytes in size.

• Accommodate changes that impacted the design, requiring modifications in over 50 percent of detailed design drawings.

Even though the initial effort in Simulation-Based Design was maritime in nature, in the winter of 1997, the focus of the program was realigned to consider applying the technology to the design and evaluation of space systems, such as the tactical support system discussed in the next chapter.

DIS synthetic environments can provide a unique tool to assist in the systems engineering process. Throughout SERCES, Zealous Pursuit, Zen Regard, and the F-15E simulator programs, there is a common thread for acquisition. The linkage is an enhanced understanding of requirements definition and operational concept evaluation for our forces. In this era of dwindling resources, when all military operations must be joint, experiments within the DIS synthetic world will let us plan and train to meet our increasing operational demands.

5

Simulation Engineering for Warfighting

As the Department of Defense continues to evolve, with the downsizing of the force structure and the shrinking of the budget, new roles and mission issues for U.S. forces need to be evaluated analytically. Historically, quantitative analytical methodologies have been used for operational requirements generation. For example, in 1993, the Chief of Staff of the Air Force directed that twenty-five-year mission area plans be developed to ensure that future operational requirements were based on analytically derived tasks and mission deficiencies.[97] Based on an examination of tactical and operational alternatives, and using traditional analysis products, the Department of Defense makes proposals for changes in the force structure.

However, one of the difficulties with the requirements process is constant modification and refinement of the underlying assumptions, based on cost variations and shifting threats. Unfortunately, these changes often take place with little or no connection to the original operational requirements. This "requirements drift" problem has serious effects on the acquisition process, eroding the credibility of the acquisition system. The use of meta-architectures[98] with linkages to DIS is viewed as helpful for mitigating these deficiencies. This total process of analytical studies, systems analysis, component evaluation, and eventual integration and testing of a final weapon system can be considered simulation engineering for warfighting. A canonical definition can be stated as follows: Simulation engineering for warfighting is the integration and utilization in simulation of any item (or key component) of the systems, weapons, equipment, processes, concepts, or tactics used by military forces, for the purpose of evaluation, trade-off, testing, or training, under operationally representative conditions other than actual combat, to determine the effectiveness, affordability, and suitability of the technologies, concepts, and tactics for application in combat by military end users.

THE PROCESS
Simulation can play an important role in systems engineering. Today, comprehensive evaluation of new warfighting systems is not possible based solely on

field integration and testing. DIS synthetic environments provide a means for decision makers and operators to realistically evaluate the effectiveness of both new and existing systems. It provides an arena for the development and evaluation of new warfighting concepts and tactics. Any warfighting system, such as sensor systems, weapons systems, intelligence and sensor information fusion processes, and command and control systems and processes, can be evaluated within a DIS virtual environment. Use of the evolving distributed simulation protocol sets and sensor modeling techniques can provide functional fidelity that is indiscernible from hardware sensors reacting to the physical environment. DIS alleviates and mitigates most real-world constraints, such as cost, security, safety, replicability of threats, limitations on use of the full electromagnetic spectrum, test instrumentation, treaty constraints, available test time, number and maturity of test articles, test maneuver space, and representative terrain and weather.

In technically complex systems, particularly when relatively small quantities of one-of-a-kind prototype elements are to be procured, insights into expected operational capabilities are needed before the complete system is available for testing. This is particularly valid in concurrent program development processes, in which all components of a system are not available, but investment decisions must be made concerning a commitment to some degree of engineering development. It is imperative that all avenues of evaluation be explored to provide a better understanding of the product when full-scale systems integration is not possible until the conclusion of the program.

Simulation provides analytical tools that augment and/or complement actual integrated system tests and provide decision makers with the necessary information to assess the progress of the acquisition program toward fulfilling the operational needs of the end user. As an adjunct to actual system evaluation, these tools can provide decision makers with valid, credible, and timely operational effectiveness, affordability, and suitability insights that would not otherwise be available. Consequently, it is appropriate to integrate simulation in the systems engineering cycle to:
- Plan and evaluate test procedures and analysis techniques.
- Evaluate partial systems before complete systems are available.
- Augment, extend, or enhance actual system evaluations.
- Develop and evaluate tactics and concepts of operational employment.
- Perform early operational assessments of expected capabilities.

The cycle encompassing the essential elements of simulation engineering is depicted in Figure 18.

Although it is true that simulation has limitations, it is equally true that waiting for end-product systems to be integrated also has limitations. For example, the number of relevant combat environments that can be addressed with minimal procured assets is limited. Together, models and simulations offer the ability to expand the operational assessment, whereas end-product demonstrations offer a more effective means to calibrate and validate the total system effectiveness.

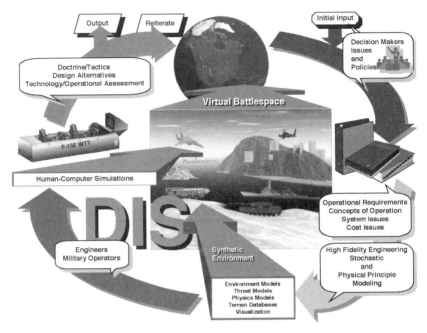

Figure 18. Essential Elements of Simulation Engineering

Although the actual product system is the preferred primary data source for operational evaluations, it may be possible to conduct only a partial replication of the expected wartime environment. It is normally not possible to complete hardware and software testing in all operational environments, with all interactions instrumented, to provide sufficient data to determine, with certitude, system combat performance. Therefore, most tests and evaluations are only partial representations of the total operational environment and at best are merely physical simulations. Nevertheless, using DIS representations of the "real world" provides additional flexibility, precision, and scope not found in other evaluation methods.

Should a decision be made to use DIS results for system engineering, caution must be exercised. For example, if DIS is used to augment, extend, or enhance other evaluation methodologies, a definitive statement should be prepared, delineating which questions and evaluation issues or parts thereof will be addressed by the DIS effort. It cannot be overemphasized that the questions and evaluation issues must be articulated before expending effort on creating a DIS experiment. It is important that both the implicit and the explicit assumptions used in DIS be carefully documented and that the risks of inexact modeling (both of the physical reality and of system interactions) be well understood.

There are certain fundamental questions to be asked whenever DIS synthetic environments are considered for use in decision making. Some of these are listed in Table 5.

In planning any DIS evaluation, it is important to understand which elements of system performance are the drivers in assessing whether or not the system meets the user's requirements. Models may be utilized to assist in the identification of those "drivers" which should be verified by other evaluation techniques.

When models are used to complement other evaluation methods or to provide early insights into system capability, it is important that the questions to be addressed be clearly defined and related to the critical operational issues. In selecting a model to address a specific question, the model should be no more complex or detailed than necessary to address the question.

Decisions concerning the use of DIS to support systems engineering should be made early in any technology investment cycle. Ideally, the user, developer, and evaluator agree up front on the models or simulations needed to provide operationally oriented assessments for the systems under consideration. An evaluation plan should be developed to transfer available generic DIS modeling capability to a mature, high-fidelity simulation for full-up system demonstration. It may not be necessary, in all cases, to develop new models or new simulations. The use or adaptation of existing simulations may be more appropriate and cost-effective. Whatever the source, the DIS environment should be consistently updated, verified, and validated with test data, field or bench measurements, and analyses to enhance predictions of real-world capabilities. Only then can the DIS synthetic environment be accredited for use in support of the analytical process.

The credibility of simulation results is a fragile commodity. Credibility, as applied to any analysis and its results, is a combined impression of the inputs, processes, outputs, conclusions, persons or agencies involved, and strength of the evidence presented. To be of use to decision makers, DIS results must be credible. The process for planning, executing, and reporting on the DIS synthetic environment should be similar to that for final integrated system demonstration. The DIS evaluation has the added requirement of providing an audit trail—with end-to-end traceability—to allow an assessment of its credibility. It is imperative that the anticipated use or development of simulation to support analysis be thoroughly documented. As changes to the DIS synthetic environment are planned and made, updates to the system engineering process should address a revised verification plan.

The following points should be considered throughout DIS synthetic environment development, implementation, and review:

Acceptability of the DIS Approach. Have decision makers involved early (and updated periodically) on a formal or informal basis.

Confidence in the Independent Models Making Up the DIS Synthetic Environment. This is based on a sound, coherent, systematic process used in

TABLE 5: DIS APPLICATION QUESTIONS

•Why was a particular component model used in the DIS synthetic environment instead of some other approach?

•Were DIS results compared with actual experience, combat,
field-test, and other models? If so, what were the results?

•Did the DIS synthetic environment accurately reflect the system
requirements and any available developmental test data?

•What was the linkage between system engineering with the DIS
synthetic environment and other traditional modeling?

•What have the results been validated against? What are the availability and source of data?

•What is the statistical confidence in the results? What sensitivity
analyses have been performed? Does the model always win
when applied? If so, why?

•Who built the component models? Who certified the inputs and
outputs? Who certified the tactics and scenarios?

•Who did the verification and validation? What implicit and
explicit assumptions were made?

•Why was each particular component model chosen? What was it
designed to do? What are its strengths or weaknesses? Where
has it been used before?

•How far has the component model been pushed to extremes, and
how has it performed? Have the DIS synthetic environment
domain limitations for the component model been established?

•Is there a documented audit trail? Will it provide traceability of
critical decisions?

---

development; a sound modeling management structure, including configuration
management; model descriptions, including usage, strengths and weaknesses,
past history, and adequate documentation; a thorough description of verification
and validation efforts; threat representation and usage; and thorough descriptions of accreditation efforts.

Confidence in the DIS Team. DIS practitioners must be experienced with
the diversity and complexity of synthetic environments, with the models being
used, and with the system being simulated. That part of the team tasked with
establishing confidence in discrete models should be independent of the developers and users of the model or simulation.

Confidence in DIS Methodology and Use. This is based on applicability or
appropriateness in addressing requirements and issues under consideration, ade-

TABLE 5: DIS APPLICATION QUESTIONS (continued)

- Is there adequate funding to support the DIS synthetic environment and experiments? By whom? Is the DIS synthetic environment cost-effective?
- What elements of the DIS synthetic environment should be confirmed by operational demonstration, evaluation, and testing?
- Were excursions made? If so, why, and what were they? What impact (if any) did excursions have on the evaluation?
- What is the degree of independence of modelers? Was an independent assessment of the applicability of the DIS synthetic environment made?
- Have the component models been used by the developers beyond the immediate evaluation context? What were the results?
- Who is maintaining the component model?
- What is the source of threat data? Is it consistent with data used in other analyses? What is the source of threat tactics used in the scenario?
- What variables of the operational environment are not represented?
- Who is expected to use or operate the component models in the DIS synthetic environment?
- Can the model be designed and built faster or cheaper than the system it represents?

---

quately described methodology and assumptions, and certified and documented input data (including scenarios).

Confidence in DIS Results. Consistency with actual system evaluation occurs when the input data used are representative of actual system evaluation conditions. Further, the results should be consistent with other test results when their input data are comparable. Any DIS results that appear counterintuitive must be fully investigated to determine whether the results are in error or whether the results actually reflect some new insight that was not previously anticipated. DIS reported results should include a description of other related evaluations, apparent inconsistencies, and any available resolution of issues identified.

DIS Verification. Verification is the process of determining whether a computer program or model performs as intended. A verification plan should be prepared for the use of DIS in the system evaluation. For new and modified models, the verification plan should describe the verification processes and the documentation for reporting verification results. For existing models and simulations, any previous verification efforts that led to accreditation should be referenced.

DIS Validation. Validation is the process that, at a minimum, addresses the following concerns: (1) the appropriateness of the discrete models in adequately answering the questions or issues under study, (2) the degree of confidence in the conclusions that can be drawn from the DIS results, (3) the appropriateness of the threat data and threat tactics used in the DIS synthetic environment, and (4) consistency in levels of fidelity between models. To be appropriate, a simulation must address critical issues with a realistic representation of the operational environment and operational context. DIS appropriateness depends on the modeling techniques, assumptions, and limitations; the input sources and quality; the ability to measure performance; and the design of the experiment. Confidence in DIS results can be enhanced by comparison with other data (e.g., actual test results, other simulations, or historical data). The sensitivity (driving and limiting factors) should be well understood and documented. Plans to recalibrate, reverify, and/or revalidate models based on actual test results should also be documented and implemented.

DIS Accreditation. Accreditation is the process of certifying that a DIS synthetic environment and its component models and simulations have achieved an established standard such that it can be applied for a specific purpose.

Figure 19 puts all these elements together. It is a stepwise methodology, with a simple beginning. The cornerstone is fundamental and absolutely essential: there must be questions to be asked or issues of concern regarding a system before the simulation engineering process is undertaken. Without system questions, requirements issues, operational concept ideas, or tactics concerns, there is no reason to enter the simulation engineering process, for there can be no useful output from the endeavor. With these things, a regimented simulation engineering approach is akin to classic scientific method: statement of the problem, formulation of the hypothesis, design of experiments, collection of data, analysis of results, and conclusions. By following this time-honored technique, the simulation engineer provides answers to system questions that could not be obtained any other way, yet have the credibility and validity to stand on their own merit.

DIS APPLICATION OPPORTUNITIES

At this point, the best approach to addressing concerns about the appropriateness of DIS as a problem-solving tool is to delineate several examples of where it can be applied. With no particular preference or precedence, these five examples are based on ongoing, pertinent efforts within the Department of Defense. As time goes by, some of these examples may become case histories of what has been accomplished.

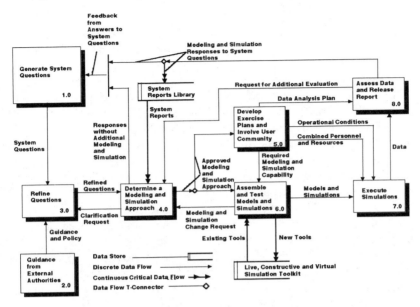

Figure 19. The Simulation Engineering Process

Operational Concept Development: Tier 2/3
Unmanned Air Vehicle Ground Station Evaluation

The Department of Defense has explored and built variants of Tier 2/3 Unmanned Air Vehicles, known by a variety of names. The Tier 2/3 Unmanned Air Vehicle flies high in uncontested battlespace, collecting massive amounts of real-time data on belligerent activity. By itself, a Tier 2/3 Unmanned Air Vehicle is an incomplete system. To function as a contributing member of the force structure in a battlespace, the Tier 2/3 Unmanned Air Vehicle must pass data to and/or be controlled by a ground station. Considerable debate hinges around whether the computer processing equipment (avionics) of the Tier 2/3 Unmanned Air Vehicle system should be airborne or should be extracted from the air vehicle, placed in a ground station, and connected to the air vehicle via high bandwidth radio (or possibly laser) data links. The trade-offs are of enormous complexity and have even greater cost ramifications.

Should the processing and avionics horsepower be on the ground or built into the air vehicle? This is a prime candidate for trade-off analysis in DIS. The testing scenario might involve the creation of a virtual battlespace with DIS human-computer simulators for intelligence collection platforms and ground stations, directing attacks by DIS human-computer simulators of fighter aircraft against DIS SimCore semiautomated forces (SimCore is discussed in detail in Appendix B).

A key aspect of any Tier 2/3 Unmanned Air Vehicle system performance is its ability to perform surveillance in the battlespace that may include 200,000 or more ground vehicles and provide that data to end users in a friendly ground station. To perform a satisfactory Tier 2/3 Unmanned Air Vehicle ground station evaluation through simulation and analysis requires a tool to generate an initial laydown of the ground vehicles and their movements over time in a computationally responsible fashion. The Rapid Scenario Preparation Unit for Intelligence (RASPUTIN; discussed in detail in Appendix B) model can be used to provide scenario setup fidelity and credibility, enabling substantive DIS analysis without compromising the design or function of the ground station. RASPUTIN can be used to generate a scenario script describing vehicle movements that can be loaded into DIS at initialization or interrogated during runtime for current vehicle state conditions. The tactics and operations of the Tier 2/3 Unmanned Air Vehicle ground station can be examined independently of the scenario generator and DIS synthetic environment.

Another significant aspect of Tier 2/3 Unmanned Air Vehicle performance is its potential to enhance strike management and the Air Tasking Order (ATO) process. Proper evaluation of a Tier 2/3 Unmanned Air Vehicle in DIS requires input from a model such as the Conventional Targeting Effectiveness Model (CTEM; described in Appendix B), which can allocate air assets across targets, providing both an allocation effectiveness assessment and the assignment inputs necessary to produce an ATO. CTEM provides the weapon delivery aircraft-target pairing assignments to create an ATO, which can also be flown and examined in Extended Air Defense Simulation (EADSIM; see Appendix B), prior to the DIS exercise. Once again, the collaboration of simulation techniques, resulting in a credible DIS synthetic environment for testing the Tier 2/3 Unmanned Air Vehicle ground station, ensures that the article under test is not altered to be part of the creation of the test environment.

Crisis Action Concept Exploration: Special Weapons and Tactics (SWAT) Team Technology Testing

Events such as the Olympic games in Atlanta, Georgia, provide a tremendous challenge to security and emergency services. The risk of international incidents from terrorism or other acts of malevolence is considerable. Successful coordination of 10,000 federal, local, and private security resources during periods of peak activity or emergencies is critical. In addition to terrorist acts, the Olympic games historically have been clouded by hostage taking, civil disorder, hooliganism, fire, transportation failures, and/or injury to large groups. For operations and the coordination of multiple agencies, events such as the Olympics provide a stressful venue.

In planning for the coordination of emergency assets for mass public events, it would be beneficial to have three-dimensional cityscapes and digital maps, detailed databases of key building interiors with SWAT team walk-through rehearsal capability, traffic and perimeter monitoring, communication networking, real-time asset tracking of police and medical personnel and vehicles, and rapid access to police databases. All these capabilities need to be on a secure network and graphically available to enable crisis management among multiple agencies in real time. One possible approach would be to replicate and enlarge on the experience of the simulation-based command and control center technologies developed by DARPA and demonstrated in the Command and Control simulation facility.[99] For example, a DIS virtual Olympic Village could be used with models of major facilities in and around the Olympic city. These could be populated with simulators for communication networks, surveillance systems, police and medical vehicles, and SWAT team systems. Scenarios could include practice coordination missions between civil agencies for search and rescue of hostages. Just such an approach was considered for the 1996 Olympics.

In the winter of 1994, thirty months before the Olympics, the FBI wrote to DARPA, requesting support in developing a field version of the Command and Control simulation facility. The FBI strongly believed that the situational awareness technologies provided by such a facility were exactly what it needed as the cornerstone for the management of security efforts in Atlanta. DARPA, however, determined that it was not in its best interest to participate in such a project and turned the FBI down.[100]

Combat Identification of Friend or Foe: Transponder Concept Exploration

In a keynote address to the Conference on Military Readiness and Technology in November 1994, the Vice Chairman of the Joint Chiefs of Staff, Admiral William Owens, suggested that perhaps the only paramount challenge facing U.S. warfighters was the difficult task of real-time situational awareness known as Combat Identification.[101] Admiral Owens suggested that in the next few years, we would see a move to equip every member of the U.S. forces with some form of active electronic identification. He pointed to new generations of satellites and the burgeoning success of global cellular phone systems as the lead-ins to a combat identification system. What Admiral Owens did not comment on were the technical hurdles of designing, building, and fielding an information infrastructure that could maintain cognizance over a million soldiers, sailors, and aircrews and all their compatriots and simultaneously provide all that information both up and down the chain of command to where it was needed, when it was needed. Such a problem is ideally suited to exploration in DIS.

One such concept to provide omniscient combat identification was proposed at DARPA. The concept drew on a synergy of off-the-shelf technology and simulation paradigms. It would consist of Dick Tracy–like individual transceivers or transponders issued to every person of concern (combatants and noncombatant supporters), linked by cellular radio frequencies to mobile and home stations attached to vehicles, aircraft, ships, command and control centers, and so forth. Each transponder would have a differential Global Positioning System (GPS) receiver, an encrypter, and a cellular radio frequency link. The transponders would have their own unique code numbers, and each user (which could be everyone in the United States) would have a unique identification code, such as his or her Social Security number and a personal identification number (PIN). To activate the system, the user inputs the identification code and PIN and a selected update rate to transmit. Foot soldiers might select one update every thirty seconds, and aircrews might select updates fifteen times per second. The computer in the transponder would use the same dead-reckoning algorithms used in DIS to determine when to transmit position updates for the individual.

One key principal to make it work is the inverse of differential GPS. A master-station concept would be defined. In any area, a master station would send out an "I am here" signal (with its own code) and an "I am listening" signal. A master station might be installed on a vehicle, in a command post, on a ship, in an aircraft, on an unmanned air vehicle, or on a satellite. Each individual transponder sends to a master station within its line of sight its user's code and PIN. The area's master station correlates all the local signals it has

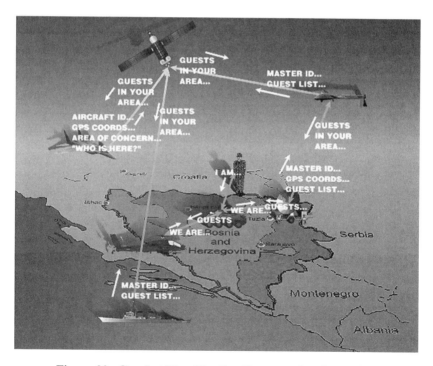

Figure 20. Combat Identification Transponder Operation

heard and compiles a guest list, with a differential position to the guests, plus its own position (see Figure 20). Then the master station seeks a higher-level master station that it has heard from and sends its own code and position and its guest list differentials, and so on, up the chain. Any individual can be subject to any master but sends data addressed only to that master. Any master can be subject to any other master that it has heard and wishes to send to. The total update rate of the system end to end is less than the error bounds of the dead-reckoning algorithms for each of the individuals.

One testing scenario could involve high-fidelity human-computer aircraft simulators (Air Force fighters and Marine helicopters) and tank simulators, with the tanks mixed in among a battlespace filled with enemy armor forces simulated by semiautomated forces. The mission of the fighters would be to provide combat air patrol to protect the helicopters, which are engaged in a search and rescue of downed aviators, while also providing close air support to the tanks. Hardware and software simulators of the combat identification transponders would be integrated into the DIS virtual battlespace. Testing would involve not only evaluation of the hardware and software systems of the transponders but also development and evaluation of the operational concepts regarding their use.

This problem is particularly sensitive to data throughput and management of database resources. The system architecture is analogous to a distributed simulation architecture. As such, it is a prime example of a warfighting issue in which all the hardware and software technologies could be developed, integrated, tested, and validated in a synthetic environment.

User Requirements Evaluation:
Tactical Support Satellite Interface Evaluation

In 1993, Congress mandated that the Department of Defense cease conducting its space business as usual and procure a Tactical Support Satellite (TSS) under new guidelines. Congress stipulated that the TSS would open new doors for requirements definition and evaluation and would be built to respond to explicit user needs. Bold new acquisition processes were expected to be used in the procurement of the TSS. The intelligence organizations that traditionally develop systems such as TSS are always reluctant to deviate from the tried and true (albeit horribly expensive) path they have always followed when building satellites, and Congress wanted that to change. One approach to encourage that change would be to use DIS throughout the development, testing, and deployment process. This could be done by using DIS to provide:
- Support to overall system and mission design goal definition.
- Support to the process of competitively selecting contractors.
- Support to system and mission concept of operations definition.
- Support to overall system engineering during the total development cycle, including test and evaluation.
- Training of future users.

In the concept development phase, which would include multiple contractors, the TSS program would evaluate, understand, and further define or evolve a definition of user needs in an operational sense. It would also assist with the definition of a methodology and criteria for the establishment of user satisfaction criteria and measures. These quantifiable criteria would be directly integratable into DIS experiments, studies, and evaluations, thereby permitting the relative scoring of a diverse set of candidate solutions. Initial studies at low- to mid-fidelity levels would focus on determining performance ranges versus return on investment for such things as target location and identification accuracy, availability, visibility, timeliness, and other criteria. All technical criteria would derive from user satisfaction criteria and measures.

For proprietary information, isolation, and security concerns, stand alone DIS simulation activity would be performed to evaluate specific models provided by the competing contractors. These models could include various algorithms that consider sensor performance operating under a variety of environmental conditions and preliminary top-level concepts of operation. Competing contractors would provide their models and the necessary technical support staff to the TSS program. The models could be interfaced to DIS simulation frameworks, such as SimCore, to provide a common engineering trade space.

During the development acquisition phase (after awarding the project to the winning contractor), the DIS effort would be conducted as more of a collaboration among the TSS program, the development contractor, and the future operational users. The DIS system engineering support would address the following areas during the development life cycle:

• High fidelity human-centered DIS environments would be used to demonstrate the baseline concept of operations to the user-consumer community, the winning contractor, and other related organizations that are partners in the TSS acquisition.

• DIS environments would be used to demonstrate, study, and evaluate the effectiveness of alternative concepts of operations. These studies would focus on developing a concept of operations that would provide the needed mix of user satisfaction and an evolving battlespace environment. Future users would be involved with the simulation engineers, systems analysts, and development contractor engineers in this process.

• The DIS environment would be applied to investigate alternative performance, cost, and risk trades as the TSS program progresses through detailed design. Prior to final implementation of a flying prototype, the DIS environment would be used to demonstrate and communicate to all relevant organizations the implementation baseline.

Each of these phases would be supported with a multitude of traditional analysis tools as well as DIS. For any program, there will be hundreds of questions that must be answered. For TSS, the more explicit details of 103 sample systems engineering issues are included in Appendix D. These issues can be addressed by one or more of six methodologies: policy-level engineering decisions, simple static spreadsheet analysis, detailed engineering numerical analysis, discrete event simulation, human-centered DIS simulations, or operational live simulation exercises. Appendix D enumerates the systems engineering issues as questions and notes what tools might be used in obtaining the answers. Of interest is that fewer than half of the questions (44 of 103) should be explored in a DIS framework. A careful reflection on these sample questions clearly articulates that not all issues can or should be evaluated using DIS. Yet it is this type of matrix of questions that must be built for any program before a decision is made to evaluate an issue in a DIS synthetic environment using human-computer simulations.

Joint Doctrine Development: The Arsenal Ship
In early 1996, the Navy and DARPA announced that they would pursue cooperative development of a future Arsenal Ship—a weapons platform capable of carrying 500 missiles. The Arsenal Ship concept is an outgrowth of the Navy's shift in focus from the open ocean to the littoral.[102] It is fully consistent with current naval doctrine as articulated in "Forward . . . from the Sea" and proposes an innovative means of providing more decisive, responsive, and varied naval support to the land battle. Through the concentration of massive firepower, continuous availability, and application of netted targeting and weapons assignment, the Arsenal Ship concept would supplement the force of aircraft carriers and Tomahawk-capable combatants and submarines. The ship would specifically be tailored to meet the heavy support challenge in the opening days of a conflict, without having to rely on the call-up of nondeployed surface ships and submarines from the United States.

The Arsenal Ship, along with other forward deployed naval and joint forces, would most likely be the key to the successful introduction and early employment of ground forces in a conflict. Initially operating under the control and umbrella of regularly deployed Aegis combatants, the Arsenal Ship concept envisions providing the Unified Commander-in-Chief with improved capability to halt or deter an invasion and, if necessary, the ability to build up coalition land-based air and ground forces to achieve a favorable conflict resolution. With a current vision of no more than a six-ship force, the Arsenal Ships would be stationed forward, near the hot spots, always available for rapid movement on receipt of even the most ambiguous or limited strategic warning. Much like maritime prepositioned forces, the Arsenal Ships would remain on station for indefinite periods without dependence on host-nation support or permission.

This future ship would act as a stand-off battle asset, deploying Tomahawk cruise missiles, theater ballistic missiles, and strike missiles designed to hit fast-moving targets ashore. A revolutionary approach to control of these naval assets is being studied as part of the evolving concept of operations for the Arsenal

Ship. The stockpile of missiles could be controlled by Army or Air Force officers. The ship could emerge as a truly joint-service platform. According to Rear Admiral D. Murphy, Director of Surface Warfare Requirements, in certain mission contexts, nearly every commander in the region could have access to the missiles aboard the Arsenal Ship.[103]

Unlike current naval operations, use of Tomahawk missiles in the region would evolve to be under the tactical control of the Joint Forces Air Component Commander. This commander is usually an Air Force general who is responsible for the daily planning of long-range strikes in the theater of operations. Similarly, missiles aboard the Arsenal Ship committed to theater ballistic missile defense would be under the tactical control of the theater air defense commander, once again, probably not a Navy officer. And the strike missiles for ground attack would be under the tactical authority of the local ground commander. Rear Admiral Murphy stated, "If we are successful in netting the command and control and weapon targeting through a single joint network, we would envision a day where a lieutenant colonel on the ground is not only calling for fire, but he is digitally directing that fire in real time. He controls the key to the weapons."[104]

This new doctrine would be a dramatic change from current operations. Today, weapons are designed and developed by each of the military Services for its own specific use. Only as an afterthought is consideration given to how to interface and interact with the other Services.

Although all the technologies exist today to build an Arsenal Ship—stealth ship design, efficient propulsion systems, maintenance, operation, logistics and weapon control automation, and real-time satellite-derived targeting intelligence—these technologies have yet to be integrated into a highly automated ship with minimal crew, built-in protection, and advanced communication networks. Key to the emergence of the Arsenal Ship are advances in command, control, and communications technologies. The networking of these technologies is critical to enabling commanders of all the Services to make use of the Arsenal Ship's assets.

The Arsenal Ship is under development through a cooperative agreement between the Navy and DARPA. Starting in 1998, an initial demonstrator ship will be built with $350 million from the Navy and $170 million from DARPA, for sea trials beginning in 2000.

The Arsenal Ship program provides the Department of Defense with a rare opportunity to perform mission evaluation, doctrine development, and perhaps even functional testing using DIS technology. As a joint-service mission satisfier, the concept clearly requires significant exploration of the interfacing and interacting among the ship drivers, arsenal maintainers, and combatant operators. The Arsenal Ship opens whole new realms of actionable command and control—who talks to whom, when, and how to employ its amassed firepower. A more tangible target for DIS could not be fathomed.

Like its DARPA program predecessors Zealous Pursuit and Zen Regard, the virtual combat program for the Arsenal Ship has a unique moniker—Zulu Abeam, a ferocious warrior standing silent abreast the shores of a conflict. And Zulu Abeam would draw on the virtual prototyping technologies and techniques developed in the DARPA Simulation-Based Design program.

The scenario for Zulu Abeam would be simple but encompassing. The Arsenal Ship would be placed in a littoral cruise amidst a burgeoning conflict between nation-states in the Middle East, eastern Mediterranean, or Southwest Asia. Zulu Abeam would encounter a well-equipped antagonist force with weapons acquired legitimately from U.S. weapon stock drawdowns and foreign military sales. Tensions would be heightened with the closure of primary sea lanes of communication and choke points.

Implementation of the scenario could be done with existing networked simulation sites. The DARPA Command and Control Simulation Center could model the bridge of the future stealth ship. It would be connected via simulation networking to the Joint Forces Air Component Commander in theater. The littoral waterborne threat and support environment could be networked from the Naval Research and Development Center in San Diego. The airborne environment could be provided by the Theater Air Command and Control Simulation Facility in Albuquerque. And the spaceborne assets would be simulated by the National Reconnaissance Office in Washington.

Zulu Abeam is an experiment that DARPA could execute today. It could pave the way for a revolutionary joint doctrine definition for the use of a naval platform of unprecedented firepower. The cost of the simulation would be minimal, but as shown in Figure 12, the payoff might be significant savings in refinement of the requirements for the Arsenal Ship. As discussed earlier, if the right questions can be formulated, and the Services are willing to ask them, DIS could provide remarkable insight into the potential employment of this future battlespace dominator.

6

New Paradigms and Ancillary Issues for DIS

As with any topic as broad as simulation, there is a propensity to try to discuss all relevant topics and paradigm shifts. For DIS, discussion would not be complete without considering architectures; verification, validation, and accreditation; and costs of simulation.

SIMULATION ARCHITECTURES

Any discussion of the architectures for DIS must address two important issues: simulation integration and the description of modeling and simulation architecture in terms that are meaningful to DIS users as well as developers.

For the first, attributes of simulations or models should provide understanding of how a wider framework for interoperability might be established or how individual elements might be modified to conform to interface standards. These attributes should address the problems of interface definitions, model resolution and scope, time handling, environmental definitions, network control, and user interaction. Compliance with the precepts of the High Level Architecture mandate may be the answer.

For the second, although the architecture dictates the way that models should behave in the overall framework, it does not dictate the methods of construction of the different models. A successful architecture is flexible enough to accommodate a wide range of models, as long as it properly handles the time and environmental constraints of the common battlespace and controls the information flow among the elements of the aggregate simulation. Given the Department of Defense's investment in DIS, model developers should take care to discuss architectural implications for simulation behavior from a user's frame of reference. The user of a model is an integral part of the human-machine dialog, and the interoperability problem begins with the need to translate freely between a user's conceptual framework and that of the model developer. Architectures must explicitly include enough detail to cut across the philosophical boundaries separating simulations from different user communities.

In terms of large Department of Defense combat simulations, particularly DIS, the term architecture refers to information formats (syntax), information content (semantics), and physical or electronic connections (networks) that join one model or simulation to another. Any architectural relationship must have at least the first two attributes—some information format and content. In the case of synchronized, real-time simulations, a direct physical or electronic connection is necessary. Description of any form of an architecture immediately becomes a matter of a design language that is commonly understood among all builders (e.g., blueprint drawings) and interface standards (e.g., specifications for bolt size, thread pitch, and torque limit). Architecture can be defined as a collection of interface standards, a common design language, and a conceptual framework for orienting discourse about model and simulation issues.

In any simulation architecture, two or more models or simulations are said to be interoperable if information flows between or among them at a rate sufficient to support normal operations of specified users. This definition recognizes that interoperability is, by nature, situation dependent. Strictly speaking, if an analyst can conveniently take several days to translate the output file from one model for input into another model and still support the schedule constraints of his or her work, the criterion for interoperability is met. However, if an integrated simulation of air and ground warfare slows down the progress of the battle to less than the training needs of the users, interoperability does not exist.

Recently, the Air Force proposed a common approach to the development of next-generation simulation capabilities. The foundation of the approach was agreement among U.S. forces to develop a joint simulation architecture for campaign-level representations of the use of military force. This architecture effort was initiated coincident with the development of the High Level Architecture of the Defense Modeling and Simulation Office and, in the long term, was directly in concert with the intent of the new common technical framework. Within the architecture, each of the U.S. forces would effectively represent its contribution to the overall battle while coordinating efforts on common issues. In the past, individual efforts were often duplicative and uncoordinated, certainly in the area of common environment and database concerns, and often in representations of the forces and operational concepts of other Services. This led to difficulty in sharing data and the results from confederations of simulations. According to the Air Force Modeling and Simulation Office:[105]

• U.S. forces develop simulation methods and tools independently, with no common standards.

• Due to this independent development, efforts have often been duplicative and have resulted in interface difficulties, data sharing problems, and overinvestment of critical simulation dollars.

• These problems will continue if current practices are continued.

In principal, U.S. forces must agree to jointly develop a common framework within which to represent their various elements. For example, SimCore exhibits just such an architecture in the form of an object-oriented environment (see Appendix B). Within this environment, U.S. forces can take the lead in supplying their force-specific objects and behaviors while coordinating efforts on common elements such as environmental descriptions (e.g., terrain), command and control constructs, and databases. Under this structure, sharing information becomes far more straightforward, and the confederation of U.S. force capabilities is a design feature rather than a post hoc effort.

The long-term goal of this approach is to integrate the range of U.S. forces missions within a common architectural framework—one that includes live, virtual, and constructive simulation capabilities and that can address training, testing, and analytical simulation needs. Some critical characteristics of any such architecture are flexibility; reliability; a non-proprietary nature; an ability to support live, virtual, and constructive elements; and an ability to address multiple levels of resolution. Part of this process is the identification of current approaches and elements that are potentially applicable to a future architecture. This provides a more disciplined development and a better focus for simulation investment. Working the simulation problems together provides for economy of scale while increasing the reliability, acceptability, and credibility of modeling tools.

VERIFICATION, VALIDATION, AND ACCREDITATION

No discussion of DIS, computer software, or simulation in general would be significant without due consideration of the software nemesis of verification, validation, and accreditation. For two decades, the validity of combat models used by the Department of Defense has been questioned.[106] One of the more recent critiques[107] was prepared by the Department of Defense at the request of Congress[108] in 1991 and resulted in the establishment of the Defense Modeling and Simulation Office and issuance of Department of Defense Directive (DODD) 5000.59. In addition, in October 1992, the Department of Defense Inspector General's report on "Duplication/Proliferation of Weapons Systems' Modeling and Simulation Efforts Within the Department of Defense" found little cross-fertilization or coordination of simulation programs within the department. The sad state of affairs concerning the verification, validation, and accreditation (VV&A) of Department of Defense models and simulations was described as follows:

> The vast majority of models and simulations currently used in the Department of Defense have not been verified, validated, or accredited. The Department of Defense has no requirement, criterion, or standard by which to accomplish a VV&A process. Weapon system requirement decisions, development decisions, engineering designs, operations, and test and evaluation results may be based on operations research data that is inaccurate or misleading.[109]

In February 1996, the Director of the Office of Test, System Engineering and Evaluation, Dr. Pat Sanders, expressed her concern over the lack of interoperability and testing of simulations:

Many simulations are developed and used in the acquisition process and consume millions of dollars every year. Many of the simulations are focused on engagement and tactical aspects of the battle. The problem is that there are too many models and simulations. The Acquisition Task Force in a modeling and simulation survey determined that there were 900 models and simulations in use, of which 600 were different. They are not interoperable, they are difficult to compare and validate, and in many cases while the program managers pay to have them developed, they do not necessarily pay to have them delivered. In short, Department of Defense pays too much for what it gets. We need some command standards, interfaces and environments to provide for interactive, reusable modeling and simulation capabilities.[110]

Establishment of the Defense Modeling and Simulation Office and issuance of DODD 5000.59 were intended to improve the practice and management of modeling and simulation within the Department of Defense, including verification, validation, and accreditation of models and simulations. These actions have had visible beneficial effects, especially in promoting joint development (or confederation) and use of models and simulations. However, verification requires man-hours, and validation requires data, many of which have to be collected in exercises and on test ranges. Both of these activities are costly. It remains to be seen whether verification, accreditation, and especially validation will be funded well enough to be fully applied. Changing the existing culture—in which validation is not considered mandatory and is often waived, with the justification that it would be too difficult—will be expensive and time-consuming.

DODD 5000.59 defines validation as "the process of determining the degree to which a model is an accurate representation of the real-world from the perspective of the intended uses of the model."

The approach to VV&A in the Services is to establish central focal points for simulation issues and to charge those focal points with oversight:

• The users of simulation products take the lead in recommending and funding specific V&V plans. The plans balance V&V level of effort, resources available, and the significance of the decisions under consideration.

• Proponent organizations for existing models, through model managers, have responsibility for coordinating and funding solid, long-term V&V programs for simulation applications and supporting databases. Proponent organizations ensure that VV&A efforts are documented and archived, so that succeeding accreditation efforts can leverage prior work.

• Future model development plans employ a continuous improvement philosophy and allocate sufficient resources toward achieving V&V goals and objectives.

Philosophically, it is essential to understand what VV&A translates into in simulator terms. General Paul Gorman suggested in testimony before Congress, for instance, the consideration of a tank simulator connected to the Defense Simulation Internet. If the purpose is to develop coordination in driving, target acquisition, and gunnery, it provides a valid simulation of combat from the perspective of its crew. This could be checked by a live simulation using real tanks, as was done in the Army's Close Combat Tactical Trainer Program.[111] There also have been efforts to validate both a virtual DIS and a constructive simulation on the basis of combat data collected during the Gulf War.[112] But according to General Gorman, the simulator may not provide a valid simulation of combat from the perspective of the loader (a crew member), if the purpose is to develop the loader's coordination and upper-body strength so that he can correctly select and quickly load fifty-five-pound rounds in a tank sprinting over rough terrain.

That shortcoming could probably be remedied at considerable expense by developing a moving base for the tank simulator, and whether it had been remedied could be checked by live simulation. But how can one tell whether one exercise, or the average of 100 exercises conducted with 100,000 netted simulators, will predict the chance of winning the next large campaign, wherever it may be? Even if one limits consideration to a handful of strategic scenarios, there are so many possible operational variables that one cannot test the validity of the simulations under all conditions of interest. Analysts have noted that "the reason for using simulation paradoxically precludes any complete validation (because we cannot afford to create the same conditions in real life)."[113] Essentially the same thing was said in a 1992 workshop on validation:

> In extremely complex and difficult modeling situations, the requirements for comparing real-world results and model results may be difficult, if not impossible, to meet. . . . Ironically enough, it is this inability to replicate (or even to understand) the real world that drives one to the use of a model in the first place.[114]

Subjective judgment must be used in the output validation of some combat models and simulations, just as it is in nuclear reactor safety assessments and space launch reliability estimates. There are rigorous methods for making subjective uncertainty explicit, quantifying it, combining estimates of different subjects, and updating the combined estimate in a logical manner when relevant data become available. One analyst who advocates such methods for validation notes that "this validation process is unquestionably subjective, but not capriciously so."[115]

With the introduction of the High Level Architecture as part of the Department of Defense common technical framework, a new paradigm in VV&A must be articulated. According to Margaret Loper at the Georgia Technology Research Institute,[116] the High Level Architecture facilitates the interoperability of all types of models and simulations. The simulation community understands that there are (at least) two steps to interoperability: simulations need to be able to exchange data, and simulations need to understand the data that are exchanged.

The ability of a simulation to exchange data via the common framework established by the High Level Architecture must be tested to ensure that the simulation is complying with the design rules and interfaces. Once the framework has been tested, the ability of the simulation to understand the data exchanged must also be tested to ensure proper operation of the federation.

To accomplish this testing, a process has been developed that consists of two phases. The first phase addresses the High Level Architecture framework—specifically, whether a simulation complies with the functional elements, interfaces, and design rules that allow it to exchange data. This is known as compliance testing. The second phase addresses the simulation's ability to understand the data and participate in a federation. This phase is called federation testing.

The compliance testing phase is to ensure that a federate conforms its actions to the interface specification, the object model template, and the simulation and Runtime Infrastructure rules as defined in the High Level Architecture (see Appendix A). Compliance is specific to each federate, not to the federation. Therefore, once a federate has passed compliance testing, it can be reused as often as needed in a federation. It is important to note that compliance testing does not guarantee interoperability; rather, it is the first step.

The purpose of federation testing is to ensure that the federation requirements are satisfied and that there is compatibility among simulations in a way that matters for the federation. Federation requirements include things such as information that needs to be exchanged, data standardization, and timing. These tests are called application and integration-level tests. Compatibility among simulations includes things such as synthetic environment representation, object representations, and conceptual model of the mission space. These tests are called functional and scenario-level tests.

As a principal portion of federation testing, developers must verify that an object generated by the federate being tested can interact with an object generated by another federate. Of primary interest is the federation object model interaction table and object interaction protocols.

Object interaction protocols are an emerging technique for describing the sequence of events and data exchanged among federates for specific types of interactions (e.g., air-to-air combat). Object interaction protocols are part of the data dictionary/protocol catalog and specify the types of attributes exchanged among federates and the correct sequence of the exchange. In this context, object interaction protocols encompass much of the existing DIS PDU work, in that DIS PDUs currently describe the data exchanged among simulations. The difference is that object interaction protocols go another step forward by specifying a standard way in which the exchange should take place.

The long-term success of DIS and the High Level Architecture depends on the simulation community embracing these precepts for VV&A. The Department of Defense has even instituted multiple on-line home pages on the World Wide Web to focus attention and expertise on simulation. Understanding the importance of top-down support, the Department of Defense has strengthened its reliance on department-level policy management and oversight of simulation. According to Dr. Sanders:

> The Executive Council for Models and Simulations, and its subordinate functional area councils, are designed to oversee the development of Department of Defense modeling and simulation policies, plans, programs, publications and procedures, such as the Department of Defense Instruction for Validation, Verification and Accreditation of models and simulations. The council is intended to encourage improved communications and coordination among Department of Defense modeling and simulation activities by fostering and supporting the Modeling and Simulation Information System and the Modeling and Simulation Coordination Center. [117]

COSTS OF DIS

It seems that every new technological adventure begins with promises of low costs and ends with the surprise of escalated financial burdens. DIS carries on the traditional polyphony of lower costs and better performance with certain ironic twists. Since simulation is a support activity and does not contribute in a Clausewitzian fashion to massive violence against an enemy, it is difficult to gauge the efficacy of cost appraisals regarding its use. Yet from the very beginning, DIS advocates have extolled the high return on investment as compared with other methods of obtaining the same goals.

In a 1988 comparison of cost versus value, *International Combat Arms* reported a fiscal proportion that has been repeated in perpetuity. The author, Douglas Nelms, cited the costs of transporting and training a battalion of armor at the National Training Center, Fort Irwin, California, at $5.6 million, with suspect training outcomes.[118] At the National Training Center, U.S. Army battalions are pitted against opposition forces who live at and train daily at the center. Usually the home team wins, and the losers leave with negative training and have little opportunity to replay and revise their actions to learn from their mistakes. Nelms suggested that with SIMNET, the battalions would be better off training at home on a facsimile of Fort Irwin for the negligible cost of the electricity to run their computers. He implied that even at $250,000 per simulator, a battalion could populate itself with simulators for the cost of a single field trip. With the added experience of training in distributed simulation, the unit would get a higher return on investment than that received for any time and resources spent in live action on a live range.

Up to a point Nelms's contentions have merit. Where his analysis is weak is the investment required to develop, deploy, support, and update simulation and its associated infrastructure. Since simulation is not an active element of the combat force, expenses accrued in the simulation life cycle are difficult to correlate with warfighting resource expenditures. Clearly, the merits of training are understood by all concerned. However, as an example of the discontinuity in simulation expenses versus training with live warfighting systems, when training is conducted with a live system and it breaks down, the mere act of repairing or replacing the system contributes directly to replenishment or sustainment of the warfighting resource pool. The replenishment of a simulation resource (replacing a broken graphics computer, for example) merely contributes to the expenditure of fiscal resources.

Taking Nelms's supposition one step farther, the act of transporting a battalion to the National Training Center for training is in itself a training exercise of utmost importance to warfighting preparation. One of the crucial elements in any war is the ability to get the warfighters where they need to be when they need to be there with all they need to have. All the tactics in all the books by all the pundits of the "dead strategists society"[119] won't help if the ammunition is back home in the warehouse. This realm of the transportation and logistics trail of warfighting is ripe, uncharted territory for DIS. But pursuing it might produce only ill-gotten gains in relation to the sunk and hidden costs of simulation.

The issue of cost savings through the use of simulation, whether for training or for acquisition, will be debated in perpetuity. Even the October 1996 "Study on the Effectiveness of Modeling and Simulation in the Weapon System Acquisition Process" concluded, "Cost savings are especially difficult to quantify and reported cost savings are often illusionary."[120] The report suggests that most often the savings would be better described as "cost avoidance"—results obtained through methods that would be more expensive if performed in a traditional fashion.

7

Cresting the Virtual High Ground: Virtual Dominance Through DIS

In recent years, we have waged war with an unprecedented allocation of weapons systems to thwart our enemies. Today, however, we must carefully consider the ancillary effects, including the effect of negative publicity, of actions taken to fulfill our desire for peacemaking and peacekeeping. Unconstrained application of overwhelming force has become contrary to our evolving political objectives and sensitivity. Now our warfighters seek maximal effect with minimal violence. Today, more than ever, our warfighting capabilities must be responsive and unambiguous in target selection and execution. Tactical necessities dictate tightly coupled joint operational command and control. These factors translate to the need for informational dominance in the battlespace of tomorrow, securing the informational high ground. It is the power of DIS that will help us acquire the skills to master the information flow that is critical to warfighting of the future—mastering virtual combat to crest the virtual high ground and achieve virtual dominance.

DIS on a grand scale began with the reliving of the Battle of 73 Easting and the Zen Regard battle in 1993. The first showed the potential of DIS for training; the second showed the potential of DIS for systems engineering. DIS for training has repeatedly demonstrated that it is worth the investment and enthusiasm bestowed on it. In contrast, DIS as simulation engineering for warfighting has faced a tremendous challenge to demonstrate an equivalent level of utility. The technology for DIS is readily at hand, opportunities for its application abound, and pundits and advocates alike assure us that if we create the right synthetic environments, the appropriate applications will follow. Although we cannot see beyond the military crest into the virtual high ground, we are actively ascending in our climb to virtual dominance.

It is the rigorous use of DIS in simulation engineering for warfighting that will let us cope with and counter the legacy of our ascent toward battlespace dominance: that waging war is an expensive way to discover operational shortfalls or to test new warfighting concepts. Virtual dominance and the very nature of DIS—an interactive, recordable battlespace—give us the opportunity to replay and evaluate our warfighting alternatives from a military vantage, as well as from the viewpoint of the scrutinizing public. Even though the methodology of combat may be changing, the tactical necessities are not. Our tactical abilities to wage war are increasingly dependent on information management—collecting and disseminating the right information to the right user at the right time. Our recent successes have largely been attributable to the command of information. But unless we can acquire and assimilate that one critical data element, when we need it, where we need it, and how we need it, we will remain information insolvent. Exploring the tenet of actionable command and control in DIS is how we can address the issue—what we should do, when, and with which information.

The surest approach is to draw on our training successes with DIS. We must use the simulations and environments created for training as our battlespace for simulation engineering for warfighting. There we can experiment with new warfighting technologies and operational concepts from a systems engineering perspective. If, in fact, a responsible analytical process is applied, then DIS has a respectable chance of becoming the quintessential tool for molding future Department of Defense acquisitions. But we must not forget the difficulties of verifying and validating DIS synthetic environments; it is imperative that we recognize that the power of DIS is that it gives us an environment in which to experiment with human interactions—actionable command and control. If we are willing to make the investment, both in fiscal resources and in intellectual commitment, DIS will provide us with a way to investigate differences in combat philosophy, at marginal cost and with ostensibly no risk.

DIS allows us to understand the relevance of actionable command and control among all the warfighters of the future: the tank commanders, the ship captains, the aircraft pilots, the armor battery commanders, the unmanned air vehicle controllers. In deliberating actionable command and control, we will learn to master the flow of information in the battlespace. As asserted by Dr. John Deutch, recently director of Central Intelligence, "All of our efforts at analysis, at modeling and simulation, point to the tremendous tactical advantage that comes when one understands where the enemy is and where the targets are." Mastery of the information flow, of actionable command and control, will help us achieve what Deutch referred to as our "singular purpose"—dominant battlefield awareness. He asserted that "dominant battlefield awareness, if achieved, will reduce—never totally eliminate—the 'fog of war,' and provide you, the military commanders, with an unprecedented combat advantage."[121] In the realm of DIS, the keynote will be virtual dominance.

Yet we must balance our enthusiasm for DIS with a certain level of skepticism. It is easy to become overly zealous in assuming that the solutions derived from simulation are the next best thing to solutions derived in war. As discussed in previous chapters, the answers derived from DIS must be measured against the questions being asked. The key point to be restated, again and again, is that it is the actionable command and control—the human decision-making processes and the data flow associated with them—that makes the technical challenges of DIS pay off. If DIS users find the synthetic environment so engaging that their cognitive processes are skewed by the pace of the moment, the "fog of war" may be mimicked by the "fog of simulation." In such an environment, we may be able to ascertain the impact of the ongoing world crises that are driving us to an ever-increasing operational tempo. Perhaps opening up the DIS synthetic environment to public observation and scrutiny, in the fashion of the Internet, would provide us with the benefit of risk reduction through public assessment of our approaches to warfighting—long before the first shot is fired in anger.

The true test for DIS will occur when a unique, otherwise insurmountable problem is solved while transcending the bounds of both training and systems engineering. Two such challenges for the application of DIS are combat identification and the Arsenal Ship. These issues draw on all the strengths of DIS described in previous chapters. A significant step toward attaining virtual dominance is to tackle and solve such issues. In doing so, the synthetic environment will be cultivated and fertilized with the tools and techniques necessary to handle all training and acquisition simulation endeavors. Of necessity, the robustness of the environment, the geophysical and visual extent of the virtual world, the veracity of the perceived visual correlation with the true visual world, the throughput of the network topology, the processing overhead issues for participants and nonparticipants, the actionable command and control elements— all the interwoven technical issues of DIS—must be resolved in establishing the context and battlespace for simulation engineering for warfighting. This could eventually translate to unquestioned information supremacy in the real-world battlespace—battlespace dominance. It can help us satisfy our need to synthesize every microdetail of warfare into the executable whole. And it should let us meet our responsibility to consider the location, action, and interaction of every participant and nonparticipant in the battlespace—soldier, sailor, aircrew member, and civilian.

Intellectual commitment to using DIS for these purposes comes when supporters and users find assurance that DIS has the validity and veracity to meaningfully represent warfighting techniques for the future. DIS proponents and users look to DIS as the method for exploring troublesome issues in:

- Joint connectivity of systems
- Timeliness and coordination of processes
- Accuracy and currency of information
- Readiness of forces
- Application of appropriate weapons

DIS applied to these problems can appear as simple—or as complex—as electronically networking together a tank, an airplane, a ship and other simulators at various locations and letting them all see one another and shoot and be shot at, all in recreations of the real world. The significance of DIS is that it amalgamates a collection of free-playing, interactive, human-operated elements of warfare. Recalling the 1992 Senate hearings on simulation, Dr. Victor Reis said of this technology that it "elevates and strengthens the collective problem solving abilities of human beings." By building on our experience in DIS for training, we can begin to study issues in command and control, weapon application, and combat identification. Using DIS, we can create an experimental battlespace to train, to fly, and to fight. This, in turn, helps amplify our ability to maintain readiness in support of today's operational tempo. Thus, in a real sense, in striving for virtual dominance, using DIS for both training and analysis, we can conclude that DIS will positively contribute to the execution of warfare.

In the long term, we must carefully marshal our expectations for the results of DIS, in concert with our allocation of resources to it. As the old saying goes, the output can be no better than the input. The creation of useful synthetic environments requires more investment and intellectual rigor than merely interconnecting simulators. Current strategies for research and development of training simulation are prudent and on target. To maximize the benefit of those expenditures, plans and resources for DIS need to be linked to the development of training simulation environments. All DIS efforts—both training and acquisition related—need to adhere to strict interoperability standards and joint architectural guidelines, with special emphasis on visualization issues. Compliance with the High Level Architecture will mechanize this endeavor. Yet, to be meaningful, all efforts to use DIS for acquisition—simulation engineering for warfighting—must be preceded by the articulation of questions and issues to be evaluated in DIS.

The alternative to this approach would have severe, perhaps irreversible detrimental effects on the use of DIS in the Department of Defense. We can expect no more out of DIS than we are willing to put into it. Lack of intellectual discipline in creating DIS technology and the underdesigning of DIS experiments would radically fracture DIS credibility. Insufficient funding of DIS research and development programs for training would force a scaling back of synthetic environment technology products, compromises on interoperability, and less collaboration in meeting joint architecture guidelines and would mitigate attempts to adopt a common visualization approach. Weakened DIS training programs would force the acquisition community to attempt to duplicate the development of synthetic environment capabilities. The diluted resources from both communities would inadequately solve the technical puzzles of creating operationally acceptable virtual battlespaces. The end result would be technical gadgetry of marginal use or interest to anyone but the developing communities.

But this doesn't have to occur. The opportunity to make DIS a cornerstone of our U.S. forces is here today. Department of Defense senior management recognizes this and is prepared to take the necessary stand. As the late Admiral Jeremy Boorda summarized in his eloquent presentation to the Interservice/ Industry Training and Education Conference in December 1994:

> As we continue to define roles and missions, it will be an evolutionary process and changes will occur. Rather than depending primarily on historical methods, like lessons learned from wars and fleet exercises, to drive these changes, virtual simulation technology offers us revolutionary new capabilities. We experiment and test new warfighting concepts, but also address anticipated needs and potential technologies to meet them. The goal, of course, is to develop concepts that will enhance our capability to win and to translate these concepts quickly into requirements, doctrine and tactics. Clearly, simulation technology appears to be a viable means to bring the right force into the 21st Century.

But Admiral Boorda also admonished us to remember that the technology itself is not the solution, but a tool to refine our mental prowess in the art of warfare:

> We must focus on sharpening our critical thinking, and wean ourselves somewhat from our fascination with technology as the answer to every situation. A finely honed human computer who outthinks his opponents is the most important capability on the [flagship] bridge of the future. While the technology revolution is indeed speeding the processing of information, the real premium for the future—as I see it—is on those who can outthink the opponent. Consequently, what matters ultimately in war is the way we combine and sequence our tactical schemes. We have an opportunity— if we seize it—to enhance our warfighting capabilities through the evolving technology of computer simulation. Technology, in fact, that is here today.[122]

Appendix A

High Level Architecture

THE HIGH LEVEL ARCHITECTURE PARADIGM

In response to the Department of Defense Modeling and Simulation Master Plan (Department of Defense 5000.59-P), the Defense Modeling and Simulation Office established a common technical framework to facilitate the interoperability of all types of models and simulations and to facilitate the reuse of modeling and simulation components. The High Level Architecture[123] was developed in accordance with objective 1-1 of the master plan, which was adopted by the Department of Defense in October 1995. HLA is one of three legs of the Department of Defense common technical framework for modeling and simulation; the other two are conceptual models of the mission space and data engineering and standards. This common technical framework represents the highest-priority effort within the Department of Defense modeling and simulation community. Initial definition of the High Level Architecture was accomplished under the sponsorship of the Defense Advanced Research Projects Agency Advanced Distributed Simulation program. The High Level Architecture baseline definition was approved by the Undersecretary of Defense for Acquisition and Technology on September 10, 1996. All Department of Defense simulation programs were required to identify their compliance plan by the summer of 1997.

Under the common technical framework and HLA, major functional elements, interfaces, and design rules can be defined, pertaining (as feasible) to all Department of Defense simulation applications and providing a common framework for specific system architectures.

The High Level Architecture does not prescribe a specific implementation, nor does it mandate the use of any particular software or programming language. Over time, as more advanced technology becomes available, new and different implementations will be possible within the framework of HLA.

The High Level Architecture is also intended to be applicable to all types of simulations and is targeted toward new simulation developments. It does not preclude application to existing legacy simulations, but it is recognized that although current systems may be able to accommodate some aspects of HLA, others may be too costly or intrusive to incorporate.

The High Level Architecture is intended to serve two sets of users—developers and policy makers—with the goal of facilitating interoperability as well as reuse.

As keeper of the faith, a High Level Architecture oversight group, called the Architecture Management Group, was formed by the Department of Defense Executive Council for Modeling and Simulation. It is made up of representatives of major Department of Defense simulation programs that have a vested interest in successful compliance with the new HLA mandate.

Programs participating in the Architecture Management Group were selected because they represented the major simulation requirements across the department, ranging from analysis to training to test and evaluation, from detailed engineering representation to campaign-level warfighting to person-in-the-loop interactive vehicle simulators. The group membership includes representatives from the following:

- Defense Modeling and Simulation Office
- Distributed Interactive Simulation
- Synthetic Theater of War
- Joint Simulation System
- Warrior Simulation for the Year 2000
- Battle Force Tactical Trainer/Naval Simulation System
- National Air and Space Warfare Model
- Joint Tactical Combat Training System
- Simulation-Based Design
- Close Combat Tactical Trainer
- Joint Warfare System
- Joint Modeling and Simulation System
- Test and Evaluation for Electronic Warfare
- Integrated Air Defense Simulation
- Leading-Edge Services for the Global Command and Control System
- Battlefield Distributed Simulation–Developmental

In examining a functional view of the architecture, the first key component consists of the federates. A federate can be a computer simulation, a manned simulator, a supporting utility, or even an interface to a live player or instrumented range. The High Level Architecture imposes no constraints on what is represented in the federates or how it is represented. The second functional component is the Runtime Infrastructure, which is, in effect, a distributed operating system for the federation. The third functional component is the interface, providing a standard way for federates to interact with the Runtime Infrastructure.

Other general capabilities of simulation systems are supported by the architecture, including the passive collection of simulation data, the monitoring of simulation activities, and interfaces to live participants, such as instrumented platforms or live command and control systems.

The High Level Architecture is structured around an object view of the world. The architecture is characterized in terms of objects, but this does not imply that development of the simulations is necessarily in an object-oriented language. The implication is that human-centered simulations interact with the manifestation of discernible real-world objects. It is the interrelationships among those objects that is the common element for HLA.

The High Level Architecture interface specification describes the access and services provided to federates. There are six categories of services: federation management, declaration management, object management, ownership management, time management, and data distribution management. Federation management services offer basic functions required to create and operate a federation. Declaration management services support efficient management of data exchange through the information provided by federates, defining the data that they will provide and will require during a federation execution. Object management services provide creation, deletion, identification and other services at the object level. Ownership management services support the dynamic transfer of ownership of objects or attributes during an execution. Time management services support synchronization of runtime simulation data exchange. Finally, data distribution management services support the efficient routing of data among federates during the course of a federation execution.

Objects are the real-world entities that are of interest in a simulation. These objects are characterized by their identity, their state, and their behaviors, and their relationships are specified through their attributes, associations, and interactions.

The key technical issues encumbering successful implementation of the High Level Architecture include the following:
• The technical viability of a single interface specification to support the wide application base of HLA.
• The technical feasibility of building a Runtime Infrastructure with the necessary range of tools needed by those applications.
• The impact of HLA on simulation internal development.
• The utility of the object model concept and formats throughout the HLA life cycle.
• The ability to specify common testing methods.
• The ability to operate the HLA federations in a secure mode.
• The ability of HLA to address the wide range of Department of Defense simulation applications.

There are five prototype implementations of federations, or "proto-federations," using the High Level Architecture to support the architecture baseline development process. The first proto-federation is called the platform prototype federation. It is a federation of real-time platform-level simulators and simulations that are current users of DIS 2.0. The second proto-federation is the Joint Training Prototype federation. It is working with the High Level Architecture to coordinate multiple discrete event simulations using the Runtime

Infrastructure time management services. It is also exploring the ability to hand off ownership of objects or attributes in a federation and is examining options for providing dynamic environmental effects across a federation.

The third prototype federation is the analysis proto-federation, called the Joint Warfare Simulation program, which incorporates two new battlespace execution models with a strategic deployment simulation prototype.

The fourth engineering prototype federation is examining the use of the High Level Architecture in simulations to support acquisition using validated engineering-level simulations and using object ownership management to hand off the computation of certain effects to selected simulation facilities to support hardware-in-the-loop applications.

The fifth proto-federation is the Joint Precision Strike Demonstration experiment. It includes a federation of other component programs such as the Modular Semiautomated Forces program and engineering-level simulations. In its original implementation, the Joint Precision Strike Demonstration program developed a customized capability, providing many of the same type of services proposed in a general form in the High Level Architecture. The Joint Precision Strike Demonstration program thus provides an excellent opportunity to assess how well HLA would work in this type of heterogeneous application environment.

The High Level Architecture requires that federates build the functionality required to interface with the Runtime Infrastructure and exchange data with other federates via the HLA specified interfaces.

Universal interoperability (the ability of any simulation to interoperate with any other simulation, regardless of original purpose or technical implementation) is not feasible with today's technology. Realistically, interoperability will be attainable in degrees, with the required level of interoperability determined by the needs of the community of common interest (i.e., the federation).

The High Level Architecture provides a common architecture for the reuse of simulations. HLA is based on the premise that no single model or simulation can satisfy all uses and users in the Department of Defense at all levels of resolution.

The memorandum signed by the Undersecretary of Defense for Acquisition and Technology on September 10, 1996, requires that all Department of Defense simulation programs use the High Level Architecture and sets out a timetable for the review of simulations and the development of migration plans. The Architecture Management Group is responsible for defining the criteria for compliance. In general, however, it is important to recognize that the goal of HLA is to provide a cost-effective approach to developing federations and reusing simulations along with the necessary supporting software. This makes HLA appealing to program managers.

It is also important that the High Level Architecture be integrated into the broader technical community. Work is under way in a partnership with the IEEE Workshop on Standards for Distributed Interactive Simulation (DIS Workshop), which is committed to establishing industry standards to support HLA. This effort was initiated at the fourteenth DIS Workshop in March 1996. The conference formally began tackling the High Level Architecture at the sixteenth DIS conference in March 1997.

THE HIGH LEVEL ARCHITECTURE PROCESS
As the principal proponents and originators of the new architecture mandate, Dr. Judith Dahmann and her counterparts described a process for implementing the High Level Architecture paradigm.

The High Level Architecture paradigm dictates that federation development begin with a user and a requirement. The federation execution sponsor is the organization that uses the results and products from a specific application of modeling and simulation. The federation sponsor is responsible for specifying the complete set of objectives to be addressed through instantiation and execution of the federation. In articulating the objectives, the sponsor stipulates the federation requirements in a formal specification "language" that is mutually understandable by both the sponsoring agency and the ultimate designers of the federation. The object is to state the problem that is to be addressed by the establishment and execution of a federation. The description of the problem domain implicit in the objective statement is critical for focusing the domain analysis activities in the conceptual analysis phase. It specifies the top-level goals of the federation and may specify the operational need or shortfall from which federation developers will derive a scenario for the federation execution. The federation developer formulates a scenario whose execution and subsequent evaluation will lead toward achieving the study objective set forth by the federation sponsor. The scenario provides identification of the major entities that must be represented by the federation; a conceptual description of the capabilities, behavior, and relationships (interactions) among these major entities over time; and a specification of relevant environmental conditions (e.g., terrain, atmospherics). Another step is to develop a conceptual view of the objects and interactions that must be supported by the federation. The primary activity in this phase is to decompose the federation scenario into explicit components (at a conceptual level) expressed as objects and interactions.

The conceptual model of the mission space is the component of the Department of Defense technical framework that bridges between the warfighter, who owns the combat process (and serves as the authoritative source for validating its content), and simulation developers. Additionally, the conceptual model of the mission space provides a common viewpoint and serves as a vehicle for communication among warfighters, doctrine developers, trainers, the command and control community, Intelligence developers, and analysts. The conceptual model of the mission space remains independent of specific applications by addressing the superset of entities, actions, and interactions occurring in any mission space, before the simulation developer makes decisions for the particular simulation to ignore, instantiate, or abstract for that development.

One of the principal activities in federation development is to identify the Object Interaction Protocols that will be required for the federation application. Given the context of the federation execution, the Object Interaction Protocols provide a standardized description of object interaction sequences and pre- and postconditions associated with certain classes of object interactions that are required to implement the functional area or areas of interest. The definitions and formats at all levels—from atomic elements to Object Interaction Protocols to families of such protocols—will be stored in a protocol catalog, envisioned as an on-line database that will contain standard definitions and formats of data exchanged between distributed simulations.

An initial version of the protocol database is being developed and populated by the joint database elements project at Fort Huachuca. The database is being seeded by data from the DIS 2.0.4 and 2.x series protocol standards. It will also be seeded with data from the Aggregate-Level Simulation Protocol 1996 Joint Training Confederation Operational Specification. In addition to the protocol database, there will be resource repositories to provide ready access to useful information for building Federation Object Models, including instance databases, conceptual models, models, and simulations. An example of an information domain supported by the resource repository is the Department of Defense data dictionary, an electronic, Department of Defense–standardized glossary of relevant terms.

A few of the significant steps in the transition from designing the overall federation to the process of fully developing the Federation Object Model are listed below:

• Reconfirm the responsibilities of the federates for representing the conceptual objects and interactions of interest.

• Establish the semantics of the federation execution through utilization of the Department of Defense data dictionary.

• Establish the relationships (associations) among the public objects, including part-whole relationships.

• For each object, utilize the attribute list currently supported by the object publisher as a point of departure.

• Obtain additional agreements among the federates regarding Federation Object Model development methodologies (with associated tools).

Finally, the conceptual-level scenario constructed during the earlier scenario development phase is instantiated at a more detailed level, complete with identification or specification of authoritative data sources for scenario components.

To make the High Level Architecture process work, certain products must be delivered. These federation products provide necessary input for the specification of the federation required execution details and Runtime Infrastructure initialization and facilitate the reuse of this information in future applications.

The public data exchange information generated during development of the Federation Object Model is recorded in the format specified by the High Level Architecture Object model template. The resulting tabular representation of the Federation Object Model provides a common, development methodology–independent means of documenting both the federation semantics (for Runtime Infrastructure initialization) and the exchange of information among the federation participants.

The object model comprises the specific classes of information resident in the High Level Architecture Federation Object Model that are required for Runtime Infrastructure initialization. At a minimum, this includes the naming of all public objects, attributes, and interactions. The execution details portion of the Runtime Infrastructure initialization data is derived by extracting the specific classes of information resident in the federation required execution details that are required for Runtime Infrastructure initialization. The execution environment is a description of the various system components that will be used to support the federation execution. These include, but are not limited to, the host computer type, configuration, network address, and location and the network components, including bit rate capabilities, latencies, multicast capabilities, and so forth. Altogether, the federation required execution details is a global specification of the classes of information needed by the Runtime Infrastructure to instantiate an execution of the federation.

Prior to actual federation execution is federation testing. It assumes that individual federates can interoperate with the Runtime Infrastructure using the High Level Architecture interface specification (i.e., they are HLA compliant before joining the federation).

The federation execution itself represents the actual operation, over time, of a subset of the federates and the Runtime Infrastructure initialization data taken from a particular federation. Assuming that the High Level Architecture process began with a properly codified set of objectives, the federation execution will produce output data that will populate the measures of effectiveness or after-action reporting data. These are the results that address the overall objectives of the execution. At the conclusion of the exercise, all output data produced by the federation execution are analyzed to determine whether the federation requirements stated in the federation required execution details have been fully satisfied.

Feedback is provided whereby the results are assessed, and the results are provided back to both the federation designers and the federation execution sponsor.

The federation development and execution process is written to provide a framework for understanding how the High Level Architecture will generally be used in the development of distributed simulation applications. In addition, it specifies how other parts of the overarching common technical framework for modeling and simulation can contribute to the design of an effective federation.

Appendix B

DIS Support Simulations and Tools

There are innumerable simulation tools available to practitioners of DIS—far too many to catalog here. Described below are a few tools that have been actively and successfully used by DARPA in early attempts at using DIS in simulation engineering for warfighting in SERCES, Zealous Pursuit, the Zen Regard exercises, and the tier 2/3 unmanned air vehicle experiments.

DEFINITIONS[124]

- A *scripted war-gaming model* executes scripted players in a tactical environment, providing no mechanism for interaction between the operator and the simulation during execution.
- A *semiautomated force*—SAFOR—is a software package that can execute scripted players in a tactical environment and allow for commander-in-the-loop real-time interaction and decision making in the analysis of command actions.
- A *framework* is a system for developing and executing a set of models of tactical players for the purpose of analyzing their capabilities and tactics in a simulated environment. Models may be person-in-the-loop, scripted, or SAFOR and may be developed at whatever level of fidelity needed. A framework is not itself a simulator but provides the functions for the execution and synchronization of models (aggregated, platform, or system models) that have been developed and/or imported into the framework.

RASPUTIN

The Rapid Scenario Preparation Unit for Intelligence (RASPUTIN)[125] is an automated, knowledge-engineered, rule-based scripting tool that allows the user to build a detailed scenario with minimal input. RASPUTIN uses expert system software to compose, deploy, and move military forces from major units down to individual vehicles in a doctrinally accurate manner. RASPUTIN may be used to construct intelligence scenarios for a variety of training and exercise support applications. The system reached initial operating capability in March 1992; version 1.2 was released in June 1993. Recently, it has been deployed at several U.S. Army installations around the world.

RASPUTIN is intended to generate detailed, doctrinally correct military deployment scenarios for collection simulators. Its software includes databases of military organizations and equipment for Blue and Red forces, geographic products, weather, and fixed sites. An expert system contains doctrinal rules used to generate correct deployments, considering force composition, terrain, road networks, slope, and weather. RASPUTIN scenarios can be used for any military application or for any scenario that can be described as placement and movement of groups of vehicles, ships, or airplanes.

RASPUTIN databases contain:

• Generic Tables of Organization and Equipment (TO&E) for Blue, Orange, and Gray ground, air, and naval forces. Generic Blue organization, equipment, and deployment doctrines are derived from U.S. military field manuals; generic Orange organization, equipment, and deployment doctrines are derived from former Soviet doctrine.

• Geographic database of National Imagery and Mapping Agency (NIMA) products for Europe, Southwest Asia, and Korea. The database incorporates terrain features at 1:1,000,000 scale and slope data at 1:250,000 scale. The data can be partitioned by geographic area. NIMA database products with terrain features at 1:250,000 scale are currently being integrated into RASPUTIN.

• Air Weather Service database of worldwide weather for the year 1988–89. The data include all weather factors contained in the source database, at a resolution of three-hour intervals and twenty-five nautical mile grids. The data can be partitioned by geographic area.

• Global fixed-site databases for ports, airfields, and military installations drawn from the Defense Intelligence Agency (DIA), Automated Installation Intelligence File (AIIF), and NIMA Automated Airfield Information File (AAFIF).

With an appropriate interface, the scenarios generated in RASPUTIN can be formatted with the specific data required for an external simulator. A script for an external simulator can be fed directly into the simulator or transferred on appropriate media. RASPUTIN currently has interfaces with the U.S. Army Tactical Simulation (TACSIM), the U.S. Army Corps Battle Simulation (CBS), and the Combat Service Support Training Simulation System (CSSTSS) for scenario initialization.

RASPUTIN is designed to be used by anyone with basic computer skills who needs to create a scenario, regardless of his or her degree of expertise with military doctrine. The scenario builder must know what size and type of force are needed, where the units will be placed and moved, how he or she wants them to behave, and when the activity will take place. A user with little military knowledge can rely on the expert system and data in RASPUTIN to produce a doctrinally plausible scenario. An experienced military scenario writer can use the system-generated solution or can tailor forces and deployments to create the situation needed.

The user can tailor forces to compose specific orders of battle by modifying the generic Blue or Orange organization, equipment, and emitters associated with equipment. Force tailoring is done on a line-and-block chart display with windows for menu choices.

Force placement is accomplished by selecting a unit, clicking on a map display at the desired location, and choosing posture, orientation, and timing from menus. Once a force is placed, the user moves it by clicking on a map display at the movement objective and indicating by menu choices movement posture, timing, and actions at the objective such as placement posture and orientation. RASPUTIN then calculates the deployment and route selections using its expert system.

Postures for ground forces include assembly, defense, road march, movement to contact, and attack. RASPUTIN uses the geographic database to determine appropriate placement locations and movement routes. For placement, the system considers linear terrain features such as roads and rivers in defining unit boundaries. For road movement postures, it considers suitable roads in selecting routes. For the attack posture, the system considers slope in selecting cross-country routes.

Postures for naval forces include port/at anchor; on station, opposed and unopposed; and in transit, opposed and unopposed. For placement and movement, the system automatically considers force capabilities for antiair, antisubmarine, and antisurface warfare, as well as proximity to land in locating ships. For naval movement, RASPUTIN automatically selects routes that avoid land.

The system places air forces in deployed posture at airfields. RASPUTIN uses the fixed-site databases to select suitable placement airfields for unit aircraft.

A user who wants to depict a different deployment can change the force placement and give specific movement parameters to the force. If the user enters a deployment that contradicts the doctrinal rules in the system, RASPUTIN notifies the user of the violation; the user may override the violation or reenter the order.

Government acceptance testing included off-line analysis of the deployments produced by the system; they are doctrinally plausible as generic placements and movements. Organizational data are intentionally generic, so that a user who needs only a basic military force can easily select one, and an expert user can tailor the generic data to his or her exact specifications. Blue or Orange doctrine for placement and movement is designed to produce the most frequently encountered deployment described in open source documents.

CTEM

The Conventional Targeting Effectiveness Model (CTEM) is a constructive optimization model that produces an optimal allocation of air assets (platforms and weapons) across ground targets, based on a list of prioritized targets, mission goals, expected air defenses, target location confidence, air asset availability, and weapon system performance. CTEM produces the equivalent of a master attack plan, defining the aircraft and ordnance assignments for each target. CTEM's output master attack plan may be further refined with specific aircraft tail numbers and flight routes to create the air tasking order. CTEM's output includes an expected value assessment of the effectiveness of the air asset allocation in negating targets. CTEM may be used to generate allocations for each campaign day or, if assets are fixed for each day, the whole campaign. Key inputs required are a prioritized list of targets and a database defining the effectiveness of each weapon against each target.

EADSIM

Extended Air Defense Simulation (EADSIM) is an analytical model of air and missile warfare used for few-on-few and many-on-many simulations. It crosses the bounds between a pure constructive simulation and a virtual one; it allows for operator manipulation of discrete elements within the simulation, but not in a purely interactive mode. It models Command and Control and communications on a message-by-message basis. Intelligence gathering is modeled to support the surface-to-surface missile artillery. EADSIM was developed by the Strategic Defense Initiative for modeling surface-to-air missiles, aircraft, artillery, communications, air bases, satellites, electronic warfare terrain, weaponry, and weapons control. These models are preprogrammed at a medium level of fidelity, with graphic interfaces to adapt them to specific platforms. For example, a generic radar model using the radar equation containing six parameters creates a model that is easy to use but does not allow changes to its fidelity. EADSIM has a large user group that provides feedback to the developers regarding new functions to be programmed into later versions. With a DIS interface, EADSIM may provide a quick and easy method of adding models into a DIS synthetic environment. EADSIM includes a two-dimensional plan view display and a crude stealth-observer display. EADSIM has an extremely complete and accurate battle forces representation, including models listed in Table 6.

EXCAP

Exercise capabilities (EXCAP) provides exercise support for command posts.[126] It has the ability to generate U.S. collection capabilities and reconnaissance tracks, schedule sensors, provide sensor fields of view, and display fixed targets and envelopes. EXCAP includes a human-centered station air mission planner used by an air staffer or a collection manager, which generates missions and

TABLE 6: EADSIM COMPONENT MODELS

- U.S. aircraft (A6, A7, A10, AN12, B52, E2C, E3A, EC130H, F111, F117A, F14A, F15, F16, F18, F4G, JSTARS, Tornado)
- Soviet aircraft (HIP, IL76, MIG23/25/27/29/31, SU17/19/24/25/27, TU16/20/22/26, YAK28)
- U.S. sensors and electronic countermeasures (APG63/65/66/68/70/71, APQ-113, APR38, APS145, APV1, AWG9, MPQ50/51/53, TPS43, generic FLIR, JSTARS, THAAD)
- Soviet sensors (Bar Lock, Eyeball, Flat Face, Foxfire, HADR, Highlark, Landroll, Long Track, Low Blow, Mig-31 Radar, Slot Back, Square Pair, Straight Flush, SUAWACS, Tibe Arm)
- Rules set for about thirty-five U.S. and Soviet air and ground systems
- U.S. communication systems
- U.S. and Soviet jammers (AN12, Badger, cub, EC130, HIP-j/k/kl, JSS1 through JSS7, POD1, POD2, POD3, R834, RGND 1 and 2, RPOD1/2/3)
- Soviet air-to-air missiles (AAMs) (2 through 10)
- U.S. AAMs (AIM7/9/54C/92A/120)
- Soviet air-to-surface weapons (AS-4/6/7/9 through 12)
- ATACMS, MLRS, bombs, chaff, flares, THAAD, Tomahawk, ALCM
- Soviet surface-to-air missiles (SAMS) (SA-3/5/8/9/11)
- U.S. SAMS (Patriot, Hawk)
- Red surface-to-surface missiles (SSMs) (SS-12B, SS1C, SS-21, SS-23, Al Hussein, FROG7, Jericho11)
- Comms protocols for ATDL1, EPLRS, HAVEQUICK, JTIDS, LINK1, NTDL, TADIL-A, B, J, UHF voice

---

sends those missions to a scenario simulator for exploitation. The intelligence generated during the course of the scenario is then disseminated via simulated AUTODIN, TRAP TRE, and/or Fleet Broadcast. Messages can be TACELINT, containing locations and parameters of hostile radars, or the results of image analysis. EXCAP is interfaced to the Synthetic Image Generation System to provide information and high-fidelity target models, which are used to synthetically generate a visual image based on terrain data and photo-texturing. EXCAP also employs gray-scale visibility, aerial photo, terrain, weather, and battle damage assessment computations for imagery.

EXCAP capabilities include modeling of GUARDRAIL, national IMINT/ELINT sensors, QUICKLOOK, Red Emitters (radars), RF-4C, RIVET JOINT, and U-2R systems, which all send out composite reports. EXCAP messages can be fed to Constant Source, Tactical Information Broadcast System, or TRAP Tactical Receive Equipment. EXCAP models are shown in Table 7.

J-MASS
The Joint Modeling and Simulation System (J-MASS) is a prototype modeling and simulation framework within which extremely detailed models of systems can be constructed and exercised. DIS compliance is limited, handling only entity state PDUs.

TABLE 7: EXCAP MODEL CAPABILITIES

- The GUARDRAIL (RV-1D) is a fully deployed airborne SIGINT system (HF/VHF/UHF) with onboard sensors that are remotely controlled from the mobile ground station. GUARDRAIL intercepts, locates (triangulates using two aircraft), and classifies targets and transmits data via its ground station to Commanders Tactical Terminals at division and corps level.
- The RF-4C is an F-4 configured for tactical reconnaissance. It may carry (at least) the AAQ-9 FLIR, AVQ-26 PAVE TACK ElectroOptic (EO) acquisition, laser designator and weapon delivery system, ATARS EO/IR (advanced tactical air reconnaissance system), AAD-5 high-performance IR scanner, and ALQ-125 RF ESM reconnaissance system.
- The U-2R is a high-flying aircraft that can carry (at least) high-powered cameras and ELINT equipment. It was designed in the 1950s to fly at an altitude of greater than 70,000 feet to get above the Soviet MIG capabilities of the era and perform reconnaissance over Soviet airspace. The U-2R evolved into the TR-1.
- RIVET JOINT is an RC-135 with ELINT capability.
- TIBS is a UHF theater-level satellite broadcast network that carries air and ground track reports from up to ten sources, among them RIVET JOINT, AWACS (via RJ), SENIOR SCOUT (via RJ), and INTEL sources.
- Constant Source is a receiver and display system that handles and displays TIBS information.

J-MASS has implemented models of SA-12 and SA-N-6 for concept testing. The benefits of J-MASS are its open system architecture and nonproprietary status.

J-MASS is oriented toward modeling electronic warfare systems with models at multiple levels of complexity, including table look-ups for low-fidelity models. The framework has a strong capability for developing models of systems and subsystems at the circuit level.

J-MASS is based on a "plug and play" architecture, which essentially means software module encapsulation. It has no integral scenario generation tool but relies on packages such as RASPUTIN for constructing laydowns, scenarios, and starting conditions. RASPUTIN helps J-MASS by running scripted model motion without engagements in a preview mode.

J-MASS utilizes a structure called the "backplane," which includes protocols and software processing that provide the mechanisms to support message communications between models. J-MASS can perform multipathing and line-of-sight collision calculations. It starts with National Imagery and Mapping Agency terrain data and adds parameters to calculate reflections and emissions. It includes message traffic between processes. J-MASS supports detailed propagation effects, both aerosols and molecular, and signal parameters that most simulations do not support, including terrain reflectivity and roughness characteristics. Winds, solar flux, ionospheric bounce, and magnetosphere effects are also included. There are both monostatic and bistatic signatures, for both radio frequencies and infrared.

The J-MASS design includes heavy emphasis on the implementation of icons to represent players and elucidates procedures whereby the user can click on icons and step through a graphic decomposition of a player's subsystems. Provision is also made for an on-line audit trail of data sources and model and scenario development. J-MASS incorporates a data dictionary, including everything from acronyms to definitions. Approved models in the database are presented so as to visually differentiate them from unapproved models. This allows a user to mix approved models with his or her own models and easily keep track of each type. Outputs include formal report files describing models and scenarios.

MODULAR SEMIAUTOMATED FORCES

DIS provides an architecture for producing large-scale simulation environments through the use of independent simulators communicating via a common network protocol. Early on, the Army made a commitment to such simulations, as exemplified by the SIMNET and CCTT programs. Within a DIS battlespace such as SIMNET, hundreds of trainees may simultaneously participate in a single simulated battle. They can see one another, communicate, move in the simulated terrain, and engage in combat. But to fight a war in a battlespace, trainees need an opposing force.

The challenge is simulating individual infantry troops and noncombatants. Infantry troops are critical to the success of most phases of land combat, and noncombatants are present in many battlespaces, especially in urban combat and low-intensity conflicts. Mission rehearsal systems have been developed for special operational forces and security personnel, but dismounted infantry troops (or units) are not simulated in networked simulations that use the DIS protocol,[127] a deficiency that critics argue makes the outcomes "predicted" by SIMNET exercises of questionable relevance to likely combat, especially the low-intensity conflict in which U.S. forces are most likely to be involved in the near future.

There are at least three ways to provide the opposing force. In the first method, two groups of trainees in simulators oppose each other. This method is often used, but it has a serious flaw, in that U.S. trainees are faced with opponents who use U.S. tactical doctrine. A second method is to use human instructors who are trained to mimic enemy doctrine. Doing so is expensive in manpower costs. The third technique is to use a computer system that generates and controls multiple simulation entities using software and possibly a human operator. Such a system is known as a semiautomated force (SAF or SAFOR) or a computer-generated force.[128]

Semiautomated forces were originated as part of the development of SIMNET. After the SIMNET development program was completed in 1989, SAF research was conducted under a DARPA project called ODIN. ODIN started with much of the same software as SIMNET but massively overhauled it and changed basic hardware platforms. A variety of different, incompatible SAFORs were built within the simulation community: BDS SAFOR, AirNet SAFOR, AGPT SAFOR and Marder SAFOR (for the Germans), MCC SAFOR, Alsemo-Net's SAFOR, and temporary versions for testing (such as the TodFor). The primary motivation for making a modular SAFOR was to combine the various groups into one generic version that could be easily customized to any customer.

MARS
The Multiwarfare Assessment and Research System (MARS) is a framework designed to encompass models that assist in the analysis of naval antiair warfare, antisubmarine warfare, antisurface warfare, strike warfare, mine warfare and electronic warfare. The antiair warfare and strike warfare areas are the most fully developed. Resolution of existing models is fairly limited: surface-to-air missile and air-to-air missile flyouts are straight lines. Electromagnetic countermeasures and maneuver effects are modeled through changes in probability of hit tables, and cross sections are point sources. Terrain data are based on National Imagery and Mapping Agency data. MARS can be run in either a scripted "engagement mode," which is designed as an analysis tool and can have multiple iterations, or in a human-centered "war-gaming mode," which allows operators to make tactical decisions.

RESA

Research, Evaluation and Systems Analysis (RESA) was designed to support research and development and training for senior naval officers, focusing on command and control of battle group or force operations. It was originally named the Battle Group Tactical Trainer and evolved into RESA in 1988 in an effort to increase research and development applications. RESA has been used for requirements analysis, technology evaluation, concept formulation, system testing, system design, architecture assessment, operational plan evaluation, command and control training, joint operations interoperability, and distributed war-gaming. RESA is intended mainly for simulation of the total naval warfare environment but includes some aspects of ground warfare. Tactical presentations include both geographic and status displays at each of up to forty command stations, which can be Red or Blue. Each operator or commander can direct his or her own forces, assign missions, deploy sensors, establish and operate comms, and receive orders and tactical tracks information.

Some specific models employed by RESA include platform kinematics, navigation, flight operations, sensors (visual, radar, electronic support measures, sonar, sonobuoy, special underwater surveillance, high frequency direction finding, over the horizon radar, satellites), jamming, communications (voice, data links, satellite laser communications), emission control procedures, track correlation, electromagnetic interference, operations (amphibious, mining, macro antisubmarine warfare), weapon engagements (gun, cruise missile, torpedoes), operations and kinematics for surface/subsurface/air platforms, battle damage, and weather conditions. Actual message formats can be generated for RAINFORM, JINTACCS, OTH-T GOLD, and the Naval Tactical Data System Link 11 and sent to internal or external systems.

RESA is one of the older distributed, human-centered simulations and has been executed under many programs, including naval, joint, allied, and DARPA projects such as SERCES.

SIMCORE

SimCore is a research and development effort of DARPA that provides a synthetic environment framework for the development and execution of virtual battle simulations. SimCore supports experimentation with system concepts and doctrine and evaluation of mission effectiveness in the context of associated battlefield systems, operating against intelligent adversaries, in various battle-space environments. SimCore builds on the DIS approach to multientity simulation, adding capabilities normally found in analytical simulation frameworks and extending the DIS concept to meet the needs of material and combat developers.

SimCore is a discrete event simulation framework. Whereas DIS provides transparency in interentity communication, the SimCore object-oriented architecture provides transparency inside of entities. SimCore retains the DIS emphasis on human-centered command and control simulation but adds capabilities such as faster than real-time operation to support Monte Carlo analysis.

SimCore provides end-to-end simulation and analysis facilities. Tools that allow developers to quickly incorporate new models and reconfigure new scenarios are provided. Automated data collection procedures and visualization and statistical analysis tools are embedded as an integral part of the architecture. Provisions for distributed entities and external data gateways allow for the incorporation of models and data from multiple sources. The flexibility to combine constructive, virtual, and live entities in one simulation extends the kinds of exercises that can be performed and provides new types of analysis capability.

The SimCore simulation framework provides a flexible, scalable, modular environment for performing and analyzing distributed operational simulations. The tactics component provides the system with a computer-generated force capability with the objectives as shown in Table 8.

SimCore supports multiple modes of operation, including simulation development and integration, systems engineering and analysis, and test support. Simulation development and integration are supported by providing an environment for the rapid development and reconfiguration of new battlefield entity simulations and the configuration of theater-level exercises using largely

TABLE 8: SIMCORE COMPONENT OBJECTIVES

- Provide a standard representation formalism for computer-generated force tactics for all SimCore applications.
- Provide a modular representation in which tactics can be constructed out of reusable software components.
- Provide a representation that is extensible in both breadth and depth, to avoid limits on the scope or fidelity of computer-generated force behaviors. The representation should also maintain a separation between tactics and platform models (physical behaviors).
- Provide for modification of tactics in real-time during execution of a simulation.
- Provide for monitoring of tactical characteristics during a simulation.
- Provide a representation of command and control.
- Provide user interfaces that aid the warfighter, the operations analyst, and the simulation specialist in the development and application of computer-generated force-controlled entities within the simulation.

computer-generated forces with some manned entities. As an aid in system engineering analysis, SimCore provides analytical trade-offs, multiple levels of fidelity, and a development platform for the evaluation of human interfaces and tactical decision aids. Finally, as part of test support, SimCore supports test planning, training, test personnel, and real-time execution monitoring with control. Although originally developed under the auspices of Zen Regard, SimCore technology has become an essential part of ongoing simulation for acquisition programs, including the Simulation-Based Design virtual prototyping program, as described in Chapter 4.

Appendix C

The Players:
Who Does What

Simulation has become an enterprise unto itself within the Department of Defense and industry. There are countless organizations and people who play significant and pivotal roles in fashioning the application of DIS and the High Level Architecture. It is impractical to enumerate them all, but a few note-worthy ones are mentioned below (see Figure 21).

In the Department of Defense, simulation is headed up under the Office of the Secretary of Defense, Director for Defense Research and Engineering. Under this office is the Defense Modeling and Simulation Office and the Defense Advanced Research Projects Agency. There is also an Executive Council for Models and Simulations to advise the Department of Defense in implementing simulation policy. On the Joint Staff (J-8) is an office that provides the Joint Chiefs with a focal point for simulation across the military Services. Each of the Services has at least one office that oversees and guides simulation activities in that Service. And there are supporting activities dedicated to helping orchestrate Department of Defense simulation, such as the Institute for Simulation and Training and the Defense Modeling and Simulation Tactical Technology Information Analysis Center. Finally, with such diverse participation, it is important to note that there is a common meeting ground where they all discourse: the DIS Conferences on Interoperability.

DIRECTOR FOR DEFENSE RESEARCH AND ENGINEERING
One of the most pivotal players in DIS was Dr. Victor Reis. Beginning in 1990, while Director of the Defense Advanced Research Projects Agency, he advocated the application of DIS to acquisition. He envisioned an acquisition process in which new programs would be prototyped in a virtual world and employed in a virtual battlespace by operational military forces in simulated warfare. Reis pursued an end-to-end approach, in which the entire acquisition program, including design, manufacture, logistics, and operations, would be worked out on computer before committing anything to paper or hardware.

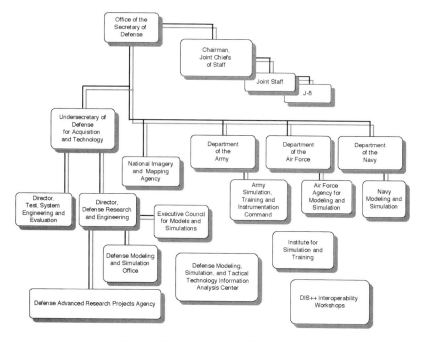

Figure 21. Simulation Who's Who

When Reis was appointed the Director for Defense Research and Engineering (DDR&E) he carried his vision for DIS with him. He created a strategic thrust for research and development to explicitly exploit synthetic environments, and he required all new research to explore the use of DIS. This top-level emphasis on simulation heralded a new age in which Department of Defense managers of all ilks were exposed to distributed simulation, most for the first time. With Reis's policy that no new research programs or funding would be approved without explicit consideration of the use of DIS, a whole new perspective on simulation was encouraged. The Air Force and Navy began to seriously investigate the potential of DIS; the Army, already well poised in DIS, used the DDR&E advocacy to support significant budget requests for training development programs such as Combined Arms Tactical Trainer.

In 1993, President Clinton appointed Dr. Anita Jones as the Director for Defense Research and Engineering, replacing Reis. Jones, who served until 1997, followed her predecessor in her steadfast support for the use of simulation. She advocated that the Department of Defense find more effective ways to implement simulation and computer technologies, in training as well as in acquisition programs. Jones tasked the Department of Defense to examine more closely the how and why of simulation as it is used today, and to find innovative applications for advanced simulation, particularly to reassess and restructure programs "that will permit us to realize more of the tremendous potential of modeling and simulation. There must be clear traceability of projects funded through the Defense Modeling and Simulation Office to both the objectives and the strategy by which it intends to achieve those objectives. Similarly, projects should cumulatively build, or at least relate, to be a critical mass in achieving objectives."[129]

The Office of the Secretary of Defense formally organized its modeling and simulation management oversight in Department of Defense Directive 5000.59 in January 1994. Within the Office of the Secretary of Defense, the Undersecretary of Defense for Acquisition and Technology is responsible for the management and advancement of Department of Defense modeling and simulation and for strengthening the uses of modeling and simulation in the Department of Defense. Working for the Undersecretary is the Director of Defense Research and Engineering. The Director is responsible for supporting the Undersecretary in modeling and simulation and for advising the Undersecretary, with the assistance of the Executive Council for Models and Simulations. This body is made up of senior representatives from the Services, the Joint Staff, and the Office of the Secretary of Defense and is chaired by the Director.

DEFENSE MODELING AND SIMULATION INITIATIVE

In May 1992, the Deputy Secretary of Defense instituted a major new initiative to strengthen the application of modeling and simulation in the Department of Defense.[130] This Defense Modeling and Simulation Initiative pertained to the joint application of models and simulations, and hence was considered complementary to those efforts carried out within the Services. Advances in the application of models and simulations led to the belief that they could make a fundamental and widespread contribution to the development and employment of U.S. military forces. Expectations of potential future capabilities included:

• Simulated warfighting environments that allow frequent and realistic joint training spanning several echelons, involving large simulated forces, and bridging large geographic areas.

• Electronic "sand tables" that provide commanders engaged in warfare with a realistic means of portraying the disposition of friendly and enemy forces and simulating the consequences of proposed courses of action.

• Simulation test beds that allow new concepts to be explored and system requirements to be refined before "bending metal" and committing to expensive developments.

• Campaign analysis models that furnish senior defense officials with a tool for budget deliberations that relates individual system effectiveness to the predicted outcome of military campaigns.

Achievement of such capabilities required a widespread, highly capable, and integrated modeling and simulation environment based on developments in the areas of architecture, methodology, and advanced technology. Many of the components of the overall modeling and simulation environment were to be furnished solely through service or defense agency developments. Given the joint perspective of the Defense Modeling and Simulation Initiative, its role was to support those aspects of the overall environment that tied together the components of individual Services or agencies or served to broaden the applicability of those components. For example, the Initiative was intended to:

• Promulgate standards to promote interoperability of the components of the modeling and simulation environment.

• Support the development of databases, tools, and methodologies for community-wide use.

• Promote the development of a communications infrastructure to support integration of joint modeling and simulation activities.

• Facilitate community-wide coordination and information sharing, emphasizing activity in three general areas: management, policy, and investment.

Objectives for each of these three areas were defined as:

• *Management:*
  1. Establish a Department of Defense–wide management structure to coordinate joint modeling and simulation activities and requirements.
  2. Promote coordination across Department of Defense components to minimize duplication in modeling and simulation development efforts and to increase productivity through combined efforts.

• *Policy:*
  1. Develop policy in specific areas necessary to ensure the effective joint application of models and simulations.
  2. Fix responsibilities to ensure the proper oversight of models and simulations with joint applicability.
  3. Furnish guidance for the consistent development of modeling and simulation plans by the Department of Defense components.

• *Investment:*
  1. Formulate and implement a long-range joint investment strategy for models and simulations.
  2. Identify and fund high-priority investments leading to enhanced joint modeling and simulation capabilities.

Within the Department of Defense, a large amount of work on a variety of modeling and simulation projects has generated multitudes of computer codes, with different designs and language implementations but frequently oriented toward the same goal. In 1992, the Defense Modeling and Simulation Initiative set out to coordinate different Department of Defense efforts to allow a degree of interoperability between existing models and simulations and to provide a framework for the seamless integration of new models. This approach built on progress in industry's open architecture solutions and DARPA-sponsored technology development in communications and hardware areas. However, higher-level application interaction was slow in coming and was impeded by a number of factors. First, no requirement was compelling enough to overcome the initial expense and programming difficulties of designing interoperable codes. Second, models were usually built to answer specific questions concerning particular studies or system developments, rather than being generalized for reuse or evolutionary growth in capability. The major goals of the Defense Modeling and Simulation Initiative were to define an architecture spanning the entire Department of Defense activity, and to foster the seamless integration of new models into combat simulations involving all components, units, and forces from all Services. In the few years since its initiation, only rudimentary progress has been made.

EXECUTIVE COUNCIL FOR MODELS AND SIMULATIONS

The mission of the Department of Defense Executive Council for Models and Simulations (EXCIMS) is to advise and assist the Undersecretary of Defense for Acquisition in implementing his responsibilities for strengthening the uses of modeling and simulation in the Department of Defense.[131] EXCIMS members are generals, flag officers, and civilians of equivalent rank and precedence. The Director of Defense Research and Engineering chairs EXCIMS meetings. The Director of the Defense Modeling and Simulation Office (discussed later) is the secretary to EXCIMS but is not a voting member of the executive council; the director's office provides administrative support for EXCIMS. EXCIMS does the following:

• Oversees the development of Department of Defense joint- and common-use modeling and simulation policies, directives, and procedures.

• Encourages improved communication and coordination among Department of Defense modeling and simulation activities.

• Identifies investments in joint- and common-use modeling and simulation that have a high-value return in fulfilling Department of Defense requirements or that fill gaps in Department of Defense modeling and simulation capabilities.

• Promotes joint and cooperative research, development, acquisition, and operation of modeling and simulation systems, technologies, and capabilities among Department of Defense components.

• Recommends Department of Defense joint- and common-use modeling and simulation goals and objectives and an investment strategy and plan to achieve them.

• Recommends Department of Defense components for designation as executive agents for general-use modeling and simulation applications, as needed.

- Fosters programs to develop and, where applicable, implement Department of Defense modeling and simulation interoperability standards and protocols.

DEFENSE MODELING AND SIMULATION OFFICE

On June 21, 1991, the Undersecretary of Defense for Acquisition, Don Yockey, established the Defense Modeling and Simulation Office (DMSO) to serve as the executive secretariat for EXCIMS and to provide a full-time focal point for information concerning Department of Defense modeling and simulation activities. DMSO reports through the Director of Defense Research and Engineering under the office of the Undersecretary of Defense for Acquisition and Technology. DMSO is responsible for developing improved communication and coordination among modeling and simulation activities and serves as the Department of Defense focal point for modeling and simulation. DMSO is also responsible for ensuring that modeling and simulation technology development is consistent with other related initiatives. In this role, DMSO supports high-leverage modeling and simulation activities of broad use to the Department of Defense community. Part of this process has been a yearly focused call for funding modeling and simulation projects. The Defense Modeling and Simulation Tactical Technology Information Analysis Center electronic bulletin board is coordinated and supported by DMSO.

Input to DMSO is coordinated through the Modeling and Simulation Working Group. The group is chaired by the DMSO and consists of senior field-grade officers who are voting representatives from those organizations represented on EXCIMS, as well as nonvoting representatives from academia, industry, and other key Department of Defense modeling and simulation developers and customers, such as the Intelligence community, the Ballistic Missile Defense Office, and DARPA.

DMSO and the Modeling and Simulation Working Group are supported by five functional working groups: (1) education, training, and military operations, (2) analysis, (3) production and logistics, (4) research and development, and (5) test and evaluation. In addition, a number of technical working groups are formed as needed to address particular topics.

The intent of DMSO is to provide leadership across the Department of Defense to:

- Encourage improved communication and coordination among Department of Defense modeling and simulation activities.
- Function as the Department of Defense focal point for modeling and simulation and ensure that modeling and simulation technology development is consistent with other related initiatives.
- Serve as the EXCIMS secretary and provide support for EXCIMS during and between meetings.

• Chair the Department of Defense Modeling and Simulation Working Group and monitor the activities of modeling and simulation–related joint, functional sub–working groups and task forces.

• Staff and distribute Department of Defense modeling and simulation plans, programs, policies, procedures, and publications.

In this context, the Director of Defense Research and Engineering sanctions DMSO to fund and support efforts within the Department of Defense with the objectives of:

• Seamlessly linking live, virtual, and constructive simulations on demand to support the operational readiness of forces.

• Applying modeling and simulation both more broadly and with increased validity throughout the Department of Defense.

• Providing authoritative representations, with appropriate scalability, fidelity, and granularity.

• Enabling interoperability of modeling and simulation supporting technologies.

JOINT STAFF

The Force Structure, Resources, and Assessment Directorate of the Office of the Joint Chiefs of Staff provides a focal point for joint models and simulations within the Department of Defense. The Joint Staff (J-8) supports a concept of core simulation expertise through centralized management and decentralized execution, called Distributed Models and Simulation (this is physically distributed but not necessarily interactively networked, so it is not the same as Distributed Interactive Simulation). J-8 envisions the connection of virtual joint model and simulation centers that develop, maintain, and use models and simulations while collaborating across nondedicated connectivity pipelines.

The joint models and simulation sites will be built around the existing modeling, simulation, and war-gaming centers, such as U.S. Transportation Command Headquarters, the Warrior Preparation Center, the Korean Battle Preparation Center, the National Simulation Center, the Joint Task Force Simulation Center, the Joint Warfighting Center, the National Test Facility, and Blue Flag. The competencies of each center will be augmented by collaborative webs of suppliers and customers, with the J-8 providing policy initiatives, technical activities, demonstration opportunities, and funding assistance.

DEFENSE ADVANCED RESEARCH PROJECTS AGENCY

The Defense Advanced Research Projects Agency (DARPA) is the central research and development organization for the Department of Defense. It manages and directs selected basic and applied research and development projects in which both risk and payoff are very high and in which success may provide dramatic advances for traditional military roles and missions and dual-use applications. DARPA operates as a separate agency under the Office of the Secretary of Defense and reports to the Director of Defense Research and Engineering.[132]

DARPA plays a unique role in developments such as simulation technology. DARPA's charter supports entrepreneurial investment in risky but potentially high-payoff technologies. In the early 1980s, the era of Ping-Pong–like video games, few people saw the potential strength of computers and television-type technologies merging to produce revolutionary low-cost, multiple-person training systems. Huge and extremely expensive simulators had been around for decades, almost exclusively for aircraft simulation. Challenging that technology paradigm was appropriate for DARPA, which often viewed its primary role as developing things that were better, faster, smaller, and cheaper. With the innovative thinking of pioneers such as Colonel Jack Thorpe, small investments were made to turn simple video games into Army armor training systems. The idea caught on, and by the late 1980s, DARPA and the Army had invested $200 million in building a series of SIMNET-connected sites for armor and aviation training simulation.

Until recently, DARPA has continued as the lead player and mentor in technology investment for simulation, seeding the simulation industry with $250 million a year among diverse simulation programs across all the Services—for training, acquisition, manufacturing, and system engineering.[133] DARPA is the one organization that can cut across all bounds of military and corporate cultural dysfunction to tackle the intensely complex diversity of DIS technology.[134]

NATIONAL IMAGERY AND MAPPING AGENCY
The National Imagery and Mapping Agency (NIMA) was established October 1, 1996, by the National Imagery and Mapping Agency Act of 1996.[135] The creation of NIMA followed more than a year of study, debate, and planning by the defense, intelligence, and policy-making communities and Congress, as well as continuing consultations with customer organizations. Because it has responsibilities to customers outside the Department of Defense, the new agency has also been designated a part of the U.S. intelligence community.

The creation of NIMA centralized responsibility for imagery and mapping, representing a fundamental step toward achieving the Department of Defense vision of "dominant battlespace awareness." The agency was created to exploit the tremendous potential of enhanced collection systems, digital processing technology, and the prospective expansion in commercial imagery.

The agency's mission is to provide timely, relevant, and accurate imagery, imagery intelligence, and geospatial information in support of national security objectives. The vision of the agency is to guarantee the information edge.

NIMA is organized around its core business processes to enable the agency to take advantage of horizontal teaming and integration activities to draw the producers and consumers of its information closer together. The creation of the agency brought together the Defense Mapping Agency, the Central Imagery Office, and the Defense Dissemination Program Office in their entirety, as well as the mission and functions of the Central Intelligence Agency's National Photographic Interpretation Center. Those organizations were disestablished on October 1, 1996. Also included in the new agency are imagery exploitation, dissemination, and processing elements of the Defense Intelligence Agency, National Reconnaissance Office, and Defense Airborne Reconnaissance Office.

Coincident with the establishment of the new agency, in October 1996, NIMA announced that it had placed its Digital Terrain Elevation Data on the Internet. The decision to make the data public was based on feedback from U.S. government agencies as well as the private sector that the product would have some benefit to scientific and environmental ventures. The data set is a uniform matrix of terrain elevation values that provides basic quantitative data for systems and applications that require terrain elevation, slope, and/or surface roughness information. According to agency officials, this version of data is a step toward a seamless, worldwide digital terrain data set. Users can copy, manipulate, adapt, or combine it with other geospatial information. This and subsequent data releases will be updated and made available on the agency's home page.

ARMY SIMULATION, TRAINING, AND INSTRUMENTATION COMMAND

The Army Simulation, Training, and Instrumentation Command (STRICOM) is responsible for technology development and system acquisition for Army material needs in the simulation arena. It is headquartered in Orlando, Florida, colocated with the Naval Training Systems Command and the Air Force Agency for Modeling and Simulation. Together, they provide a center for the simulation development community and were the originators of the interoperability workshops—the first attempt at jointness in the simulation domain.

Although program management for DIS within the Army is at Orlando, the majority of functional DIS effort is focused on activities being conducted in what is referred to as the DIS confederation. The full confederation is still being determined; the principal core Army DIS facilities are the mounted warfare test bed at Fort Knox, Kentucky, the aviation test bed at Fort Rucker, Alabama, the land warrior test bed at Fort Benning, Georgia, and the Operational Support Facility (OSF) located in Orlando with STRICOM. The OSF provides software and configuration management support to the other three facilities. Collectively, these facilities are the Army's primary battlefield distributed simulation–development test-bed facilities, employing virtual simulators to conduct experimentation, testing, demonstrations, and "what-if" drills in support of concept development, training development, research, development and acquisition, acquisition reform development, advanced concept requirements, advanced technology demonstrations, top-level demonstration, and material development.[136]

Army simulation is guided by a strategic simulation plan outlining future investments to ensure that training remains fully integrated with the Services' goals.[137] The strategic simulation plan belongs to STRICOM Directorate Z and focuses simulation efforts through the year 2010. STRICOM intends to become intimate with future Army weapon systems requirements to ensure that training systems meet the unique demands of specific new systems. Ultimately, many of the training functions will be built into the future weapon systems themselves.

NAVY MODELING AND SIMULATION

On January 3, 1995, Assistant Secretary of the Navy Nora Slatkin issued a memorandum for the Navy to establish a rigorous and regimented simulation policy. Her memorandum stated:

> The expanded use of models and simulations has enormous potential to enable better use of valuable resources and to improve the way we acquire future weapons systems. We must build upon existing modeling and simulation capabilities and exploit emerging technologies. The Department of the Navy will use the appropriate level of modeling and simulation to support all phases and milestone decisions of the acquisition cycle. Each Acquisition Coordination Team shall strive for consensus on models and simulations to be used. As a goal, models and simulations used in system acquisition should interface with the common architecture and standards developed by the Department of Defense. At milestone decisions, the integrated program summary will describe current and future modeling and simulation efforts. The acquisition decision will provide guidance regarding the appropriate level of modeling and simulation outputs needed to support the program's next milestone decision.

Within the Navy structure, the Undersecretary of the Navy is the senior official in the Department of the Navy dealing with modeling and simulation. The Undersecretary provides guidance to strengthen the uses of modeling and simulation in the Department of the Navy. The Undersecretary is assisted by the Modeling and Simulation Advisory Council, cochaired by two executive agents (Director, Space and Electronic Warfare, Office of the Chief of Naval Operations—N6, and Commanding General, Marine Corps Combat Development Command), who direct the Department of the Navy Modeling and Simulation Management Office. That office:

• Is composed of the Policy and Coordination Office and the Technical Support Group.

• Is headed by a director and an assistant director, one from each Service (Marine colonel and Navy captain). The director routinely moves up from assistant director midway through a normal assignment. This ensures a balanced command representation for each Service, over time. The director heads the Policy and Coordination Office.

• Coordinates modeling and simulation plans (including Navy and Marine master plans and investment plans), programs, policies, and procedures across functional areas, to ensure an effective and efficient approach to the development and use of modeling and simulation.

• Maintains instructions and establishes standards as necessary to manage the Department of the Navy modeling and simulation program. It provides guidance in the development of Department of the Navy programs such as cataloging; verification, validation, and accreditation; classification mediation; and others in which a single Department of the Navy policy is determined to be required.

The Technical Support Group is headed by a civilian technical director, under the Director and Assistant Director of the Department of the Navy Modeling and Simulation Management Office, and is hosted within the Space and Naval Warfare Systems Command (SPAWAR). The Technical Support Group provides technical advice and assistance in the execution of modeling and simulation activities throughout the Department of the Navy. Specific tasks include:

• Supporting Department of Defense, Joint Staff, and Department of the Navy modeling and simulation cataloging efforts by maintaining an automated naval modeling and simulation master catalog, acting as naval point of contact for input into defense catalog systems, and providing catalogs in electronic format on request.

• Providing management of the Department of the Navy verification, validation, and accreditation process.

• Advising on standards to be used.

• Assisting in the selection and development of modeling and simulation applications.

• Building common services, tools, and databases for future development.

• Supporting development of the multiservice common simulation framework and necessary infrastructure and tools, such as common interface units, catalogs, and so forth.

• Assisting in the design of distributed simulation exercises.

The Department of the Navy Modeling and Simulation Management Office establishes working groups and task forces to assist in the accomplishment of assigned tasks. These organizations serve as extensions of the office for the discussion of issues and policies and the sharing of modeling and simulation techniques and technologies. The Department of the Navy Modeling and

Simulation Management Office provides information on modeling and simulation applications, standards, and databases managed by the Department of the Navy to the Department of Defense Modeling and Simulation Information Analysis Center. The Navy's plans for interoperability include:

• All modeling and simulation applications designated for joint and combined uses will meet Department of Defense, joint, and combined Service interoperability criteria. Developers of interoperable models and simulations will give due regard to the DIS or other approved standards during the modeling and simulation design process. Developers of models and simulations that involve representations of the functions of other Services or government agencies will coordinate those representations with the Service or agency involved to the extent practicable, as determined by the responsible Department of Defense component.

• As the Defense Simulation Internet and other interlinking communications become available, modeling and simulation applications originally developed for single Service use will frequently be employed in joint configurations, regardless of original intent. These configurations will model joint employment or compare systems to support the development and acquisition processes. For this reason, modeling and simulation developments intended for single Service use should also give due regard to DIS or other approved standards during the modeling and simulation design process.

AIR FORCE MODELING AND SIMULATION

The U.S. Air Force has long been a pioneer in the use of simulators, from the early days of the Link simulation in 1936 to today's interactive dome flight simulators. The Air Force led the way with the introduction of high technology into modeling and simulation. In April 1993, the Chief of Staff of the Air Force, General Merrill McPeak, realizing the critical importance of modeling and simulation technology, prescribed the establishment of the Directorate of Modeling, Simulation, and Analysis (AF/XOM). AF/XOM served as the single point of contact for Air Force policy on modeling, simulation, and analysis activities until 1997. AF/XOM focused Air Force modeling and simulation efforts to ensure the continued development of the most advanced and cost-effective modeling and simulation tools to support the warfighter. Some of the most powerful tools for Air Force simulation are its war-gaming centers, including Blue Flag, the Warrior Preparation Center, and the Air Force Wargaming Institute.

In June 1996, the Air Force opened the Air Force Agency for Modeling and Simulation in Orlando, Florida, collocated with the other Services' simulation offices. The agency is responsible for seeking new technologies that will pay major dividends for the Air Force in budget savings and readiness, using simulation to immerse warfighters into the environment in which they will fight.[138] The agency's mission is to implement policy, support simulation operations, and coordinate and manage simulation initiatives.

In January 1997 the Air Force merged AF/XOM into a new directorate for command and control, under the Air Force Chief of Staff for Air and Space Operations. The merger reflected a recognition within the Air Force of the convergence between the technologies of modeling and simulation and the capabilities required by command and control.

INSTITUTE FOR SIMULATION AND TRAINING
The Institute for Simulation and Training was established at the University of Central Florida, Orlando, to provide a central clearinghouse for simulation technology. Whether it was the proximity to the largest simulation complex in the world (Disney World) or merely fortuitous, very early in the burgeoning age of video games, the state of Florida recognized that simulators and simulation were technologies unto themselves. Viewing a simulator as a device that uses sounds and sights to make participants feel like they are experiencing an actual situation (with video games being good examples of low-end simulators) and simulation technology as the capability to recreate experiences, Florida foresaw that simulators held great potential for training people for almost any situation.

Over the years, with government and industry working independently with new technologies and hardware, a discontiguous range of simulations and related applications was developed. However, because of the independent nature of the developments, early research efforts were sporadic and often redundant. Researchers from agencies across the country needed better communication in order to benefit from the latest advances. They also needed a common source of academic studies to support their own work. In consideration of these needs, Florida established the Institute for Simulation and Training (IST) at the University of Central Florida in 1982. IST is located in the Central Florida Research Park next to the university campus in Orlando. The Naval Training Systems Center, the Army Program Manager for Training Devices, the Marine Liaison Office for Trainers and Simulators, and the Defense Training Performance Data Center are located near and supported by IST. In addition, more than 140 simulation and training companies have facilities nearby in the central Florida area.

For the past several years, IST has been funded by STRICOM and the DMSO to develop standards for the interoperability of distributed simulations. IST has taken several steps required in the development of DIS standards. The first step has been to host workshops and to have working groups discuss user-community requirements and to recommend methodologies to meet these requirements while addressing technical issues associated with interoperability. When issues require more practical data, studies are performed and the results presented to the working groups for comment and recommendation. When enough information is obtained to make specifications for a standard, a draft document is written and resubmitted to the working groups for approval. Since August 1989, workshops on standards for the interoperability of distributed simulations have been held twice a year. The result of these workshops and numerous interim working group meetings has been the IEEE approval of a standard containing the use and content of data messages called Protocol Data Units required for the networking of visual interactions and entity information within DIS.

DEFENSE MODELING AND SIMULATION TACTICAL TECHNOLOGY INFORMATION ANALYSIS CENTER

The purpose of the Defense Modeling and Simulation Tactical Technology Information Analysis Center (DMSTTIAC) is to fulfill the functions of a full-service information analysis center focused on modeling and simulation information sharing, including acting as a clearinghouse of information and operating an electronic bulletin board for the modeling and simulation information system. The DMSTTIAC provides scientific and technical information and support services to government, industrial, and academic communities in the areas of tactical warfare and modeling and simulation technology. The DMSTTIAC is sponsored by the DMSO and the Defense Technical Information Center and is jointly operated by Battelle and the University of Central Florida, Institute for Simulation and Training.

The heart of the DMSTTIAC is access to databases containing thousands of documents, pictures, and other material dealing with the technologies and research involving live, virtual, and constructive modeling and simulation. The database is continually updated, expanded, and refined in support of current and anticipated requirements. Potential information and data sources include technical reports from the Department of Defense, other government agencies, industry, and academic institutions; open literature, including domestic and foreign; unpublished papers; and proceedings from conferences, symposia, and workshops.

The DMSTTIAC maintains a node on the Defense Modeling and Simulation Information System, with direct connection to the Internet. This node provides access to a wide array of modeling- and simulation-related data, including details on over 1,300 Department of Defense and U.S. forces models, electronic conference mail reflectors, and an extensive calendar of modeling and simulation events. The DMSTTIAC's objective is to facilitate communication concerning modeling and simulation technology to improve the capability of U.S. forces. The DMSTTIAC applies scientific, engineering, modeling and simulation, and acquisition disciplines to support operational needs of the Department of Defense, civilian agencies, and other users in their conduct of modeling and simulation. Through the IST focus, the DMSTTIAC provides the capability for the Department of Defense, industry, academia, the public sector, and others to share information on modeling and simulation related to the technologies of Distributed Interactive Simulation and Advanced Distributed Simulation.

The DMSTTIAC provides technical support to the Defense Modeling and Simulation Office, U.S. forces, and Joint Chiefs of Staff with respect to collecting, processing, reviewing, analyzing, summarizing, and disseminating appropriate scientific and technical information and analyses. The intent is for the DMSTTIAC to provide short-term support on urgent matters when early starts and quick responses are vital and when the resources of the DMSTTIAC can offer national advantages in the performance of specific efforts.[139]

DIS CONFERENCES
For one week, twice a year, more than 1,000 scientists, engineers, trainers, and others converge in Orlando, Florida, to work together to define the technical constituents of DIS. The DMSO, STRICOM, and the IST sponsor this series of technical workshops to discuss standards for the interoperability of distributed simulations. These workshops are the meeting place for myriad denizens of the simulation world. The DIS conference has grown from its meager beginning in 1989, with attendance measured in tens of people consisting of a few technically interested and qualified engineers, to the more than 1,000 attendees today, including engineers, marketers, and government customers, as well as commercially interested artisans.

The DIS conference is the forum for technical interchange on every issue regarding distributed simulation. It ranges from highly technical discussions on the specific details of simulation implementations to more esoteric philosophical considerations of who should be in charge of verification and validation of simulator behavior. The depth and content of the conference have improved over the years, albeit at the added burden of increased membership and the ensuing decision-making overhead.

The DIS conference is supported by a number of functional area subgroups that operate throughout the year. Much of the interaction, discussion, and resolution of technical simulation issues is done via electronic communication. DMSO and IST both have Internet servers that provide a repository for data exchange on conference proceedings.

The DIS conferences are an impressive array of intellect and energy. From the early-morning coffee, donuts, and bytes to the wee-hour brews stewing over flashes of inspiration, there is an intellectual fervor unparalleled at other conferences. The DIS conferences are a working, collaborative experience, drawing together an amorphous community—with no single purpose but with a mutual direction to further the technical capabilities of DIS. The DIS conferences are an amazing investment in mental horsepower—working every minutia from the smallest details of "bit-field" structures for data interchange to the largest issues of international network communications infrastructure.

In the spring of 1997, the DIS conferences formally took up the mantle of DIS++ as their rite of passage for support of the High Level Architecture mandate.

Appendix D

TSS Question Matrix

In the table below, there are six methods of issue exploration, labeled A through F:

- A—policy decision
- B—spreadsheet
- C—engineering analysis
- D—discrete event simulation
- E—human-computer simulation
- F—operational exercise

Only the items marked with a large "X" under column E should be considered issues to be explored using DIS. Although this table was created specifically with the Tactical Support Satellite (TSS) in mind, many of the issues are common to any system that collects data and distributes it to an end customer. A table of issues such as this could be applied to other satellite or unmanned air vehicle programs.

TABLE 9: TSS SYSTEM ENGINEERING QUESTIONS

	TSS Questions	A	B	C	D	E	F
1	Is there an ultimate user for an objective?	X					
2	Who is (are) the end user(s)?	X					
3	If the data are or will be available from another source, what is the difference in timeliness to the end user?	X	X	X	X		
4	Are these data currently acquired via some other method?	X	X	X	X		
5	How does a user determine or measure mission success or failure?	X					
6	How does each user plan to use the data provided?	X					
7	How reliable are the data?	X	X	X			
8	Should this system be designed to cooperate with other systems to improve performance?	X	X			X	
9	What are the communications architectures under consideration?	X		X			
10	What are the shortfalls in the way these data are currently acquired?	X	X				
11	What are user complaints regarding the current method of data acquisition?	X	X				
12	What is the concept of utilization for each mission objective?	X					
13	Will this be used as an experimental or as an operational asset?	X					
14	Are store-and-forward and direct downlink modes required?	X		X	X		
15	Are there any availability or reliability constraints?	X					

	TSS Questions	A	B	C	D	E	F
16	How many areas of interest need to be supported simultaneously?	X					
17	How quickly does the end user(s) need the data?					**X**	X
18	If there are multiple mission objectives, is there a priority?	X					
19	What are the signal characteristics (frequency, modulation, radiated power, duty cycle, radiation pattern, and so forth) associated with each objective?	X	X	X			
20	What are the target frequency ranges?	X	X	X			
21	What data content, form, and format are required by each user?			X		**X**	X
22	What data does the user want?	X	X	X			
23	What frequency accuracy is required?	X	X	X			
24	What geolocation accuracy is required?		X	X	X	**X**	
25	What is the acceptable data latency?				X	**X**	X
26	What is the acceptable worst-case outage interval?	X	X	X			
27	What is the area of interest?	X					
28	What is the desired revisit rate?		X	X			
29	What is the expected performance life of the satellites?	X					
30	What is the maximum allowable time for calibration on orbit?				X	**X**	
31	What is the minimum acceptable revisit rate?				X	**X**	
32	What are mission objectives?	X					

	TSS Questions	A	B	C	D	E	F
33	How are data to be delivered (tactical relay, direct downlink, both)?	X	X	X			
34	Is graphic display of the data required?	X				**X**	X
35	What communications resources does the user have or need?	X		X		**X**	X
36	What is the expected TRAP config-uration for the relevant time frame?	X					
37	Will additional physical equipment be required at the workstation?	X		X		**X**	X
38	Will existing delivery systems be adequate to provide timely delivery of data to the end user?			X	X		
39	Will existing delivery systems be available when this system is to be deployed?	X					
40	Will existing equipment need to be modified to acquire and display these data?	X		X		**X**	X
41	Will tasking, acquisition, and processing of these data overburden the user(s)?					**X**	X
42	Will the person who tasks the satellite be overburdened with the responsibility?	X				**X**	X
43	Are cross-links required?		X	X			
44	Are the decision-making elements automated, semiautomated, or manual?					**X**	
45	Are there intermediate thresholds in the accuracy vs. mission utility effectiveness (MUE)?			X	X		
46	At what force level should tasking be accomplished?	X				**X**	X

	TSS Questions	**A**	**B**	**C**	**D**	**E**	**F**
47	Can geographic separations between areas of interest be accommodated?	X		X		X	
48	Can the data be transferred over existing communication channels to other users?	X	X	X			
49	Can the data be used by multiple users at the same time?				X	X	X
50	Can the target data be used by other users in different geographic locations?				X	X	
51	Does the user want to have dynamic control over the type of data to be obtained, or is his requirement stable?					X	X
52	How are requests for tasking prioritized? Who is the decision authority?	X				X	X
53	How does the coordination between user needs and tasking take place?					X	X
54	How does the network change as a function of peace, crisis, conflict?	X					
55	How does the user verify accurate reception of tasking given?					X	X
56	How does the user verify quality of data received?			X		X	
57	How is downloading to be performed?			X			
58	How are these data combined with other data to improve the overall intelligence product to the user? How is this best performed?	X			X	X	X
59	How many users in the field should be given tasking authority?	X				X	X
60	How will the system interface or interact with national systems?				X	X	

	TSS Questions	**A**	**B**	**C**	**D**	**E**	**F**
61	If store-and-forward mode is required, how much data must be stored before being downloaded?			X	X	**X**	
62	Should all data be fully processed or a combination of processed and unprocessed?			X			
63	Does the user have a chain of command governing his actions, or should he have autonomy for his actions?					**X**	
64	Was the level of security of the data a hindrance in delivering it to the end user?					**X**	X
65	What are the characteristics of each node in the network?			X			
66	What are the communications system characteristics of these nodes?			X			
67	What are the decision-making elements in the data flow path, and are they automated, semiautomated, or manual?					**X**	
68	What are the inherent problems with interfacing data from this system to "operational, validated" data from national systems?				X	**X**	X
69	What are the nominal time delays introduced by each decision-making element?		X	X	X		
70	What are the potential conflicts with these communications systems (i.e., are they used for other purposes, and are there scheduling priorities to be considered)?					**X**	

	TSS Questions	A	B	C	D	E	F
71	What exists in the community now that could be reused in some fashion—software, hardware, procedures, management structures, facilities?	X					
72	What is the capacity and utilization of each link?			X			
73	What is the data flow network?			X			
74	What is the mechanism for coordination of tasking from numerous sources within a theater of interest?	X				**X**	X
75	What is the most efficient asset command and control architecture?				X	**X**	
76	What is the sensitivity relationship between data accuracy and mission utility effectiveness (MUE)?			X	X		
77	What is the extent of the user's area(s) of interest?	X					
78	What level of security is required for tasking of the asset?	X				**X**	X
79	What level of security will the asset's products be delivered at?	X					
80	What level of security is required for transmission of data to the user?	X				**X**	X
81	Where is the optimum insertion point for the data?			X	X	**X**	
82	Which nodes are capable of receiving TSS data?			X			
83	Who is the tasking authority?	X				**X**	X
84	Who will receive processed data?	X				**X**	X
85	Who will receive unprocessed data?	X				**X**	X

	TSS Questions	A	B	C	D	E	F
86	Will cooperative tasking and data collection between TSS and other tactical assets improve the accuracy and usefulness of the data, and is this feasible?					**X**	
87	Does the user want to have dynamic control over the type of data to be obtained, or is his requirement stable?	X					
88	Are the data delivered to the end user (cockpit) timely enough to be useful?				X	**X**	X
89	Is the revisit time sufficient to be of significant value to the end user(s)? Is one system sufficient to satisfy the end user(s)?					**X**	X
90	Must the area be covered in total with a swath, or can swaths be incrementally pieced?			X	X		
91	Were the data provided by the system the right kind of data to aid in targeting or in conserving resources?				X		
92	What conditions or constraints are imposed by each objective?	X					
93	What is the minimum acceptable mission duration?			X	X		
94	What system trade-off areas can be offered by the user(s)?					**X**	X
95	How do atmospheric conditions affect accuracy of data?			X			
96	How long does it take to calibrate the system once in place?			X			
97	If store-and-forward mode is required, how much data must be stored before being downloaded?			X			

	TSS Questions	A	B	C	D	E	F
98	What advanced technologies can be used without raising risk to an unacceptable degree?	X					
99	What atmospheric compensations can or should be implemented?			X			
100	What level, if any, of on-board processing is required?			X			
101	What needs to be measured in order to determine signal type?			X	X		
102	What is the proposed launch vehicle, and is this a hard requirement?	X					
103	What orbit is most highly desirable?	X		X			

Endnotes

1. Captain H. R. McMaster, "Recreation of the Battle of 73 Easting," DARPA videotape, 1991.
2. F. Berry, Jr., "Re-Creating History—The Battle of 73 Easting," *National Defense,* November 1991.
3. V. Reis, testimony before Senate Armed Services Committee Hearings on Modeling and Simulation, May 21, 1992.
4. P. Gorman, testimony before Senate Committee on Armed Services, Department of Defense Authorization for Appropriations for Fiscal Year 1993 and the Future Years Defense Program, hearings, serial no. 102-883, part 1, May 21, 1992, pp. 673–730.
5. So enamored of the technology were the members of Congress that after the 1992 Senate Armed Services Committee hearings, Senator Strom Thurmond asked General Gorman to answer the following question for the record: "I would imagine that if you could model political and economic factors, you could make simulators for crisis management training as well. Have you recommended any analysis in this area?"

General Gorman replied, "My experience makes [me] a strong supporter of simulation as a way of preparing for future crises. That same experience leaves me doubtful that we will ever be able to adequately model political and economic factors. . . . Modeling war is comparatively simple. Battle outcomes, after all, are rooted in fairly discrete physical phenomena, and we are now well versed on how to allow humans realistically to interact with simulations of these phenomena."

Gorman's pessimism concerning crisis games echoes the skepticism expressed by RAND analyst Robert A. Levine as early as 1964, when he said "If gaming is used, any research conclusions should stand and be defended entirely on the basis of non-game 'real-world' evidence." Even with the unquestionable hype attached to DIS, both Levine's point and Gorman's response were not atypical of the GIGO (garbage in, garbage out) perspective of most computer aficionados. The concern has been expressed by simulation naysayers within the Department of Defense that no amount of verification and validation of any simulation can ever ensure precise and consummate replication of human behavior. The Senators were politely told that there are some things better left unsimulated. Some would argue that the actual issue is model building.

In counterpoint, per comments from Professor T. Jacobs, National Defense University, May 1995, "We build models in our heads and operate on them. We build models on computers and operate on them. In both cases, the paradigm is to test the model against real situations and then assess the precision with which the model-predicted outputs correspond to real events (where these can be found). The crucial point is to know what the precision is, and then use the model with a full understanding of its power—or lack thereof. In this respect, the paradigm calls for a successive refinement of the model, and thus the paradigm is a tool for discovery of operating variables that are hard to quantify, such as leadership in battle simulations."

6. U.S. Department of Defense, Office of the Undersecretary of Defense for Acquisition, Defense Science Board, "Report of the Defense Science Board Task Force on Simulation, Readiness, and Prototyping: Impact of Advanced Distributed Simulation on Readiness, Training, and Prototyping," January 1993, p. 6.

7. B. Brodie, *Summary of "On War," Carl Von Clausewitz* (Princeton, NJ: Princeton University Press, 1989), p. 642.

8. Graduation address by the director, Central Intelligence, Dr. J. M. Deutch, National Defense University, June 1995, extracted from www.cia.gov, June 1995.

9. D. Nelms, "SIMNET—Army War-Game Network" (quoting Air Force Colonel Jack Thorpe, DARPA program manager for SIMNET), *International Combat Arms,* November 1988, pp. 22–26.

10. R. Holzer, "ACTD Effort May Boost 2010 Plan," *Defense News,* May 13–19, 1996, p. 33.

11. The idea of "getting the first ten battles under their belts" arose during the Korean War, when it was found that pilots that survived ten air battles (dogfights) were much more likely to survive successive engagements. Programs such as the Air Force Red Flag exercises were instituted to give the pilots their first ten battles of "live" (simulated) air-to-air combat under friendly terms.

12. "The Battle of 73 Easting," DARPA videotape, 1991.

13. Admiral J. Boorda, Chief of Naval Operations. "Synthetic Warfighting—or—Beam Me up Scotty," Interservice/Industry Training and Education Conference, Orlando, FL, December 1994.

14. A. Jones, "Challenges for the Future," DDR&E speech on analysis and simulation, extracted from www.dmso.mil, January 1997.

15. "Virtual Reality and Technologies for Combat Simulation," U.S. Congress, Office of Technology Assessment, background paper, OTA-BP-ISS-136 (Washington, DC: U.S. Government Printing Office, September 1994), p. 11.

16. A. Jones, "Challenges for the Future," DDR&E speech on analysis and simulation, extracted from www.dmso.mil, January 1997.

17. L. Skibbie, "Joint Training Requires Budget, Effort and Technology Assist," *National Defense,* November 1994, p. 2.

18. G. de Briganti, "Higher-Tech Simulators Could Dominate Future Market," *Defense News,* April 22–28, 1996, p. 10.

19. M. Stytz, "Virtual Reality Research and Development Projects from the U.S. Government," *Virtual World,* November/December 1994, p. 48.

20. J. Dahmann, D. Ponikvar, and R. Lutz, "HLA Federation Development and Execution Process," DMSO white paper, extracted from www.dmso.mil, January 1997.

21. R. Adams, "The Realities of Simulation," *Armed Force Journal International,* December 1996, pp. 34–36.

22. A. Patenaude, "Study of the Effectiveness of Modeling and Simulation in the Weapon Acquisition Process," final report, October 1996, extracted from www.acq.osd.mil, February 1997.

23. Historically, commercial computer software has been sold in boxes containing "everything you need" to make it work: software disks, manuals, installation instructions, warranties, all wrapped up in plastic—shrink-wrapped. The connotation is that shrink-wrapped commercial software is (relatively) well validated and bug free, is covered by warranty, and is guaranteed to operate as advertised. Until the 1990s, when the

Department of Defense began to incorporate "commercial off-the-shelf" software, Department of Defense software could rarely be considered shrink-wrapped.

24. L. Long, "Time Enough for DIS," presentation for Interoperability and Standards Conference, Orlando, FL, March 1994.

25. Institute of Electrical and Electronic Engineers, *IEEE Standard Glossary of Computer Graphics Terminology,* IEEE standard 610.6-1991 (Piscataway, NJ: IEEE, 1991).

26. Excerpts, "Visual Testbed," Institute for Simulation and Training, extracted from www.tiig.ist.ucf.edu, November 1994.

27. Definitions from Department of Defense Directive 5000.59, "DOD Modeling and Simulation (M&S) Management," January 1994.

28. Interestingly, "SimCore" doesn't stand for anything. It was a label scribbled on an airplane cocktail napkin by the DARPA program manager during his creation of the Zealous Pursuit/Zen Regard simulation programs.

29. Institute of Electrical and Electronic Engineers, *IEEE Standard Glossary of Computer Graphics Terminology.*

30. T. Mastaglio, "Networked Simulators and Computer-Supported Wargame Simulations," Proceedings of the 1991 IEEE International Conference on Systems, Man, and Cybernetics, Charlottesville, VA, October 13–16, 1991, vol. 1, pp. 303–307.

31. C. Karr and E. Root, "Eagle/DIS Interface," *Proceedings of Elecsim 1994: Electronic Conference on Constructive Training Simulation,* edited by R. Smith (conducted on the Internet, April 11–May 27, 1994), extracted from ftp.mystech.com, February 1995.

32. Ibid.

33. "Virtual Reality and Technologies for Combat Simulation," U.S. Congress, Office of Technology Assessment, background paper, OTA-BP-ISS-136 (Washington DC: U.S. Government Printing Office, September 1994), p. 4.

34. C. Null and J. Jenkins, *NASA Virtual Environment Research, Applications, and Technology* (Washington, DC: National Aeronautics and Space Administration, 1993).

35. "Virtual Reality and Technologies for Combat Simulation," U.S. Congress, Office of Technology Assessment, background paper, OTA-BP-ISS-136 (Washington, DC: U.S. Government Printing Office, September 1994), p. 22.

36. DARPA was known as ARPA between 1993 and 1996; the word "Defense" was removed from its name by President Bill Clinton in 1993 but was added back in 1996.

37. Excerpts, "Defense Modeling and Simulation Initiative," May 1992, extracted from dmso.dtic.dla.mil, November 1994.

38. Excerpts, "Dead Reckoning," Institute for Simulation and Training, extracted from www.tiig.ist.ucf.edu, November 1994.

39. Excerpts from DIS Standard 2.04 draft, extracted from www.tiig.ist.ucf.edu, November 1994.

40. "Virtual Reality and Technologies for Combat Simulation," U.S. Congress, Office of Technology Assessment, background paper, OTA-BP-ISS-136 (Washington, DC: U.S. Government Printing Office, September 1994), p. 71.

41. E. Kroll, *The Whole Internet,* (Sebastopol, CA: O'Reilly & Associates, November 1993), pp. 19–30.

42. IP addresses should not be confused with electronic mail (E-mail) addresses, which are a separate issue related to domain names.

43. The IP address scheme is actually a binary 32-bit number, displayed as four 8-bit chunks. A binary 8-bit number can have a value between 0 and 255, thus the addresses range from 0.0.0.0 to 255.255.255.255.

44. As the Internet grew into an international network, individual countries needed to retain responsibility for their own domain-named computers. As such, a two-letter code as the rightmost domain name is the country code. The United States has the country code "us," but it usually isn't used or needed.

45. M. Stytz, "Virtual Reality Research and Development Projects from the U.S. Government," *Virtual World,* November/December 1994, p. 50.

46. Defense Simulation Internet site map, extracted via gopher from gopher:// triton.dmso.mil.:70/40/twg/dsi/site-map/dsi-map, June 1995.

47. The success of the Defense Simulation Internet is somewhat fogged by misconceptions and misinformation. It was built by DARPA as an experiment but was sold to users as a communication infrastructure. End users expected an operational utility equivalent to telephone service, electric power, or cable television, with their inherent reliability and availability. DARPA viewed the Defense Simulation Internet as a bold technological adventure, like a moon landing or an experimental flight-test airplane, with each day bringing a new experiment, and success measured by learning from failures rather than by offering service. The Defense Simulation Internet required significant dedicated labor to keep it running and was plagued by line outages, single point failures, software bugs and incompatibilities, hard-coded throughput limitations, and high overhead costs. As a result, in the early 1990s, many users turned away from the Defense Simulation Internet for intersite simulator connectivity, including DARPA's own Zen Regard. Zen Regard established its own dedicated wide-area network using commercial telephone T-1s, centered on the DARPA Command and Control simulation facility in Arlington, Virginia. The network used in Zen Regard set a new standard for simulation network connectivity, with over 99 percent availability, reliability, and throughput. As a result of the Zen Regard experience, DARPA stepped back and endeavored to reengineer the Defense Simulation Internet, and by the STOW-E demonstration in November 1994, it had ascertained solutions for many of the shortcomings. However, total resolution of Defense Simulation Internet deficiencies would require replacing nearly everything except its name.

48. DIS Steering Committee, "The DIS Vision, a Map to the Future of Distributed Simulation," version 1, IST-SP-94-01 (Orlando, FL: University of Central Florida, Institute for Simulation and Training, May 1994).

49. Ibid.

50. "Virtual Reality and Technologies for Combat Simulation," U.S. Congress, Office of Technology Assessment, background paper, OTA-BP-ISS-136 (Washington, DC: U.S. Government Printing Office, September 1994), p. 59.

51. Ibid.

52. DIS Steering Committee, "The DIS Vision, a Map to the Future of Distributed Simulation," version 1, IST-SP-94-01, (Orlando, FL: University of Central Florida, Institute for Simulation and Training, May 1994).

53. J. Jacob, "The Difference Between Perception and Reality," DISAM SAM-O-95, speech, Wright-Patterson Air Force Base, July 1995.

54. S. Meadows, "High Fidelity Simulators Synthesize Cockpit Drills," *National Defense,* November 1994, pp. 28–29.

55. Excerpts from "Contingency Visualization Planning Support," *Issues in Air Force Simulation and Analysis,* January 1994, extracted from dmso.dtic.dla.mil, December 1994.

56. T. Nash, "Modern Visual Systems," *Defense News,* April 1996, p. 8.

57. The World Reference Model has been identified as the DIS reference architecture for visualization databases. It was created in advanced graphics led by Dan Brockway of Science Applications International Corporation in the DARPA Simulation Engineering and Modeling development effort. It was first documented by Brockway in April 1994 and was formally submitted as an architectural process to the DIS working groups in Orlando in March 1995.

58. DMA Technical Report—Department of Defense World Geodetic System 1984, DMA 8350.2, September 1991.

59. Terrain Mapping Program Office WWW Home Page, Defense Mapping Agency, http://164.214.2.53:8001, June 1996.

60. National Imagery and Mapping Agency Fact Sheet, extracted from www.nima.gov, dated October 25, 1996, retrieved February 1997.

61. "Virtual Reality and Technologies for Combat Simulation," U.S. Congress, Office of Technology Assessment, background paper, OTA-BP-ISS-136 (Washington, DC: U.S. Government Printing Office, September 1994), p. 62.

62. D. Brockway and M. Weiblen, "World Reference Model," 12th Workshop on Standards for the Interoperability of Distributed Simulations, Orlando, FL, March 1995, vol. 1, pp. 239–245.

63. D. Nelms, "SIMNET—Army War-Game Network," *International Combat Arms,* November 1988, p. 21.

64. Ibid., p. 24.

65. Ibid., p. 22.

66. Ibid., pp. 22–26.

67. The low fidelity of SIMNET visuals has been its single greatest detractor over the years. Typical comments range from pilots describing it as video game–like and cartoonish to complete dismissal of distributed simulation by one Air Force general on the basis of "I've seen SIMNET; didn't like its looks then, don't want it now." This is evident in the mottled, quiltwork effect of SIMNET terrain when seen from aircraft simulators.

68. The hardware limits for SIMNET visuals were imposed based on the action range of the combatants, their visual horizon, and the time it would take them to traverse out of their terrain region. For ground traffic, this was adequate. It translated to a 3.5-kilometer visual horizon for ground vehicles and a 7-kilometer visual horizon for Apache helicopters and A-10 aircraft, as well as an altitude ceiling on the order of 1 kilometer. This meant that other flying vehicles could quickly outfly their apparent visual horizon or be above a permanent cloud deck, unable to see the ground.

69. D. Nelms, "SIMNET—Army War-Game Network," *International Combat Arms,* November 1988, p. 92.

70. R. Williams, "Army Simulation Provides Competitive Training Edge," *National Defense,* November 1994, pp. 24–25.

71. R. Holzer, "Larry Lynn May End DARPA Efforts on Simulation," *Defense News,* May 13–19, 1996, p. 50.

72. S. Meadows, "Integration Efforts Mold Information Technology," *National Defense,* October 1994, p. 26.

73. M. Stytz, "Virtual Reality Research and Development Projects from the U.S. Government," *Virtual World,* November/December 1994, p. 49.

74. Excerpts from "DARPA's Synthetic Theater of War," *Issues in Air Force Simulation and Analysis,* April 1994, extracted from dmso.dtic.dla.mil, December 1994.

75. Ibid.

76. R. Holzer, "Larry Lynn May End DARPA Efforts on Simulation," *Defense News,* May 13–19, 1996, p. 50.

77. "ACTD Master Plan Synthetic Theater of War," STOW program status white paper, extracted from www.dmso.mil, January 1997.

78. V. Grimes, "Navy/Marine Corps Team Changes Training Focus," *National Defense,* November 1994, pp. 26–27.

79. "DMA Factsheet—New System Let Pilots 'Fly' Over Bosnia Before Takeoff," extracted from http://164.214.2.53/Information/DMA_NEWS, June 1996.

80. J. Miller and K. Reitinger, "Force XXI—Battle Command," *Military Review,* July–August 1995, p. 6.

81. Ibid.

82. P. Sanders, "Study of the Effectiveness of Modeling and Simulation in the Weapon Acquisition Process," foreword of final report, October 1996, extracted from www.acq.osd.mil, February 1997.

83. Synthetic Environment for Requirements and Concepts Evaluation and Synthesis (SERCES) Technical Report on Exercise, Documentation and Processes, DARPA, October 1992.

84. The linear system engineering process follows a path from requirements definition to system creation to delivery of the product to the customer for use. There is generally no feedback mechanism for the customer to effect changes in the product based on satisfaction criteria until after it is finished and delivered.

85. SERCES was created to bring a sense of order to the confused world of unmanned air vehicles, joint program offices, multiservice labs, and the simulation business—a real circus. It is believed that the term *synthetic environment* may have been created and popularized as part of this acronym.

86. M. Hammond, D. Graham, and E. Kerlin, "History of the DARPA Synthetic Environment for Requirements and Concepts Evaluation and Synthesis (SERCES) Program," IDA D-1429, Institute for Defense Analyses, November 1993.

87. Ibid.

88. "DARPA Zealous Pursuit," videotape, December 1992.

89. The Zealous Pursuit Exercise Overview and Lessons Learned," Defense Advanced Research Projects Agency, March 1993.

90. C. Kanewske, "System Engineering and Evaluation," presentation for Infrared Technology Conference, Albuquerque, NM, May 1993.

91. H. Zimmerman, "Distributed Simulation Technology," draft DARPA videotape, June 1994. Zimmerman designed and built the Command and Control simulation facility, drawing on his experience as the set designer for Paramount's *Star Trek—The Next Generation* and *Deep Space Nine.*

92. P. Cooper, "USAF Pursues Virtual C2 System," *Defense News,* September 19–25, 1994, p. 30.

93. S. Meadows, "High Fidelity Simulators Synthesize Cockpit Drills," *National Defense,* November 1994, pp. 28–29.

94. The DARPA F-15E Weapons and Tactics Trainer was originally conceived in 1991 as the "knowledge acquisition prototyping testbed-aerospace node." It was intended to provide a new DIS approach to cockpit simulation for the evaluation of pilots' reactions to various levels of fidelity in cockpit simulators. It evolved into the DARPA F-15E Weapons and Tactics Trainer under the Zealous Pursuit and Zen Regard simulation efforts. With significant skepticism, the Air Force declined to participate in the program. The program proceeded within DARPA, bereft of most internal and all external support. Yet the eventual success of the program exonerated the necessity for entrepreneurial freedom within unique organizations such as DARPA. Had the program been forced to respond to written and sanctioned requirements and process or internal and external constituency approval, it would never have been built.

95. "Simulation Based Design Program Vision," excerpted from www.darpa.mil, extracted February 1997.

96. A. Patenaude, "Study of the Effectiveness of Modeling and Simulation in the Weapon Acquisition Process," final report, October 1996, extracted from www.acq.osd.mil, February 1997.

97. Excerpts from "The Meta-Architecture: A Solution for Requirements Drift," *Issues in Air Force Simulation and Analysis,* April 1994, extracted from dmso.dtic.dla.mil, December 1994.

98. A meta-architecture is typically a static software description of an organizational process, such as the generation of an air tasking order.

99. C. E. Munger, "Distributed Simulation Technologies," DARPA videotape, Draft, June 1994.

100. Author's personal notes, March 1994.

101. Admiral W. Owens, keynote address to the Conference on Military Readiness and Technology, Washington DC, November 3, 1994.

102. "The Arsenal Ship Program Vision," excerpted from www.darpa.mil, extracted February 1997.

103. R. Holzer, "Commanders May Share Arsenal Ship Assets," *Defense News,* June 17–23, 1996, p. 10.

104. Ibid.

105. Excerpts from "Simulation Architectures," *Issues in Air Force Simulation and Analysis,* January 1994, extracted from dmso.dtic.dla.mil, December 1994.

106. "Virtual Reality and Technologies for Combat Simulation," U.S. Congress, Office of Technology Assessment, background paper, OTA-BP-ISS-136 (Washington, DC: U.S. Government Printing Office, September 1994), p. 67.

107. P. Davis and D. Blumenthal, "The Base of Sand Problem: A White Paper on the State of Military Combat Modeling," RAND note N-3148-OSD/DARPA (Santa Monica, CA: RAND Corporation, 1991).

108. U.S. Congress, Senate Committee on Appropriations, Senate Report SR101-521, pp. 154–155.

109. Excerpts from "Directions in Verification, Validation, and Accreditation of Models," *Issues in Air Force Simulation and Analysis,* January 1994, extracted from dmso.dtic.dla.mil, December 1994.

110. P. Sanders, "Presentation to the George Washington Chapter of the International Test and Evaluation Association (ITEA)," September 1995, published in the *Major Range Test Facility Base Gazette,* vol. 7, no. 1, February 1996.

111. P. Gorman, testimony before the Senate Committee on Armed Services, Department of Defense Authorization for Appropriations for Fiscal Year 1993 and the Future Years Defense Program, hearings, serial no. 102-883, part 1, May 21, 1992, pp. 673–730.

112. W. Christenson and R. Zirkle, "73 Easting Battle Replication—A JANUS Combat Simulation," IDA P-2270 (Alexandria, VA, Institute for Defense Analyses, September 1992).

113. J. Freedman and S. Starr, "Use of Simulation in the Evaluation of the IFFN Process," North Atlantic Treaty Organization (NATO) Advisory Group for Aerospace Research and Development (AGARD) Conference Proceedings no. 268 (AGARD-CP-268), presented at a meeting of the Avionics Panel, Paris, France, October 15–19, 1979.

114. D. Giadrosich, "Validating Models and Simulations," *Simulation Validation Workshop Proceedings (SIMVAL II)*, edited by A. Ritchie, (Alexandria, VA: Military Operations Research Society, April 1992).

115. P. Davis, "A Framework for Verification, Validation, and Accreditation," *Simulation Validation Workshop Proceedings (SIMVAL II)*, edited by A. Ritchie (Alexandria, VA: Military Operations Research Society, April 1992).

116. M. Loper, "HLA Testing: Separating Compliance from Interoperability," Georgia Tech Research Institute white paper, extracted from www.dmso.mil, January 1997.

117. P. Sanders, "Presentation to the George Washington Chapter of the International Test and Evaluation Association (ITEA)," *Major Range and Test Facility Base Gazette,* vol. 7, no. 1, February 1996.

118. D. Nelms, "SIMNET—Army War-Game Network," *International Combat Arms,* November 1988, p. 23.

119. Clausewitz, Douhet, Sun Tzu, Mahan, Hart, and others.

120. A. Patenaude, "Study on the Effectiveness of Modeling and Simulation in the Weapon Acquisition Process," final report, October 1996, extracted from www.acq.osd.mil, February 1997.

121. Graduation address by the Director, Central Intelligence, Dr. J. M. Deutch, National Defense University, June 1995, extracted from www.cia.gov, June 1995.

122. Admiral J. Boorda, Chief of Naval Operations, "Synthetic Warfighting—or—Beam Me up Scotty," Interservice/Industry Training and Education Conference, Orlando, FL, December 1994.

123. The background on the High Level Architecture was extracted and derived from the Defense Modeling and Simulation Office World Wide Web site and two specific white papers: "Annotated Briefing on the Department of Defense High Level Architecture for Simulation," Defense Modeling and Simulation Office, extracted from www.dmso.mil, September 1996; and J. Dahmann, D. Ponikvar, and R. Lutz, "HLA Federation Development and Execution Process," DMSO white paper, extracted from www.dmso.mil, January 1997.

124. Conceptual Design Analysis Technical Report, Distributed Interactive Simulations (DIS) Survey for Applications, Space Applications Corporation, subcontract no. ETA-SD-0003-93, April 25, 1994.

125. M. Raker, "RASPUTIN: An Automated Scenario Scripting Tool," *Proceedings of Elecsim 1994: Electronic Conference on Constructive Training Simulation,* edited by R. Smith (conducted on the Internet, April 11–May 27 1994), extracted from ftp.mystech.com, February 1995.

126. Author's personal notes, October 1996. Over the years, there has always been considerable infighting in the intelligence community about ownership of models of national capabilities. Competing organizations hawked their own models as the grail for representing national systems, yet each model was often guarded under a cloak of security, so that no other organization could evaluate or use it. With the massive reorganization of the intelligence community in the spring of 1996 and the formation of the National Imagery and Mapping Agency, these turf battles came to an end. EXCAP was retired, the National Exercise Simulation System (NESS) was canceled, and the surviving National War-gaming Simulation (NWARS) was to be recreated under the guise of the National Simulation (NATSIM). The author contends that "a rose is a rose. . . ." Regardless of the eventual name and organizational owner, the capabilities extant in EXCAP will be reincarnated in the descendant simulation, it is hoped in a more extensible and robust object-oriented construct in concert with the High Level Architecture mandate.

127. Institute of Electrical and Electronic Engineers, "IEEE Standard for Information Technology—Protocols for Distributed Interactive Simulation Applications, Entity Information and Interaction," IEEE Standard 1278-1993, (Piscataway, NJ: IEEE, 1993).

128. Excerpts, "Intelligent Simulated Forces," Institute for Simulation and Training, extracted from www.tiig.ist.ucf.edu, November 1994.

129. Excerpts from "DMSO Focused Call Update," *Issues in Air Force Simulation and Analysis,* April 1994, extracted from dmso.dtic.dla.mil, December 1994.

130. Excerpts, Defense Modeling and Simulation Initiative, May 1992, extracted from dmso.dtic.dla.mil, November 1994.

131. Charter of the Department of Defense Executive Council for Models and Simulations (EXCIMS), draft, May 1992.

132. Defense Advanced Research Projects Agency (DARPA) information brochure, 1994.

133. R. Holzer, "Lynn May End DARPA Efforts On Simulation," *Defense News,* May 13–19, 1996, p. 50.

134. Author's personal notes, June 1996. DARPA has been in the high-risk, bluesky business since it was inaugurated after the Soviet launch of *Sputnik* in the late 1950s. DARPA has tackled some technology domains repeatedly. Prime examples include the recurrent theme of air vehicles, manned and unmanned. Although they all seem to crash, no matter how many hundreds of millions of dollars DARPA spends on them (witness both Have Blue F-117A prototypes and the DarkStar Stealth unmanned air vehicle), DARPA keeps coming back for more, doing more air vehicle research and development. According to *Defense News,* Dr. Larry Lynn, Director of DARPA, "is not a big fan of simulation. He doesn't think that is leading-edge stuff. He thinks that it is not a DARPA mission"(ibid.). The author's contention is that no one but DARPA can integrate and cross-pollinate DIS technology.

135. National Imagery and Mapping Agency fact sheet, extracted from www.nima.gov, dated October 25, 1996, retrieved February 1997.

136. *DIS Newsletter* 1:1 (July 1994), p. 9.

137. R. Holzer, "U.S. Army Drafts Strategic Simulation Plan," *Defense News,* May 6–12, 1996, p. 22.

138. Air Force News Service, "New Agency to Work Modeling and Simulation," *Washington Internet Bulletin,* May 21, 1996.

139. Excerpts, "DMSTTIAC," extracted from www.dmso.mil, November 1996.

Glossary

absorbing Markov chain model A Markov chain model that has at least one absorbing state and in which it is possible to get to at least one absorbing state from every state. See also *absorbing state.*

absorbing state In a Markov chain model, a state that cannot be left once it is entered. Contrast with *nonabsorbing state.*

accreditation The official certification that a model or simulation is accepted for use for a specific purpose.

accuracy The degree of exactness of a model or simulation, with high accuracy implying low error.

activity In discrete event modeling and simulation, a task that consumes time and resources and whose performance is necessary for a system to move from one event to the next.

activity-based simulation A discrete simulation that represents the components of a system as they proceed from activity to activity; for example, a simulation in which a manufactured product moves from station to station in an assembly line.

Advanced Distributed Simulation (ADS) A set of disparate models or simulations operating in a common synthetic environment in accordance with DIS standards. The ADS may be composed of three modes of simulation—live, virtual, and constructive—which can be seamlessly integrated within a single exercise. See also *constructive simulation; live simulation.*

affected attributes The specific attributes of an object class instance whose value in a federation execution may be affected by that instance's participation in a dynamic interaction with another object class.

aggregate To create an aggregated entity from individual entities. Contrast with *deaggregate.*

algorithm checks A rigorous verification of the mathematics of an algorithm to ensure freedom from any errors in the expression (e.g., incorrect signs, incorrect variables applied in the equations, derivation errors) and to ensure that the algorithms are consistent with their stated intents.

analog simulation (1) A simulation that is designed to be executed on an analog system. (2) A simulation that is designed to be executed on a digital system but that represents an analog system. (3) A simulation of an analog circuit. Contrast with *digital simulation.* See also *hybrid simulation.*

analytical model A model consisting of a set of solvable equations; for example, a system of solvable equations that represents the laws of supply and demand in the world market.

application level The layer of the open systems environment reference model (ISO 7498) that provides the means for the simulation exercise to access and use the network's communication resources. See also *open systems environment.*

Application Programmer's Interface (API) A library of function calls that allows a federate to interact with the Runtime Infrastructure.

association A type of static relationship between two or more object classes, apart from class-subclass or part-whole relationships.

attached part A visible part of a simulated entity that may or may not be present; for example, a bomb on an aircraft wing section.

attribute A named portion of an object state.

attribute ownership The property of a federate that gives it the responsibility to publish values for a particular object attribute.

battlefield view See *entity perspective.*

battlespace The three-dimensional battlefield.

benchmark Comparison of modeling or simulation results with an accepted representation of the process being modeled.

best-effort service A communication service in which transmitted data are not acknowledged. Such data typically arrive in order, complete, and without error. However, if errors occur, nothing is done to correct them (i.e., there is no retransmission).

black box model A model whose inputs, outputs, and functional performance are known, but whose internal implementation is unknown or irrelevant; for example, a model of a computerized change-return mechanism in a vending machine, in the form of a table that indicates the amount of change to be returned for each amount deposited. Also called input/output model. Contrast with *glass box model.*

boundary condition The values assumed by the variables in a system, model, or simulation when one or more of them is at a limiting value or a value at the edge of the domain of interest. Contrast with *final condition; initial condition.*

broadcast An addressing mode in which a Protocol Data Unit is sent to all DIS nodes on a network.

built-in simulation A special-purpose simulation provided as a component of a simulation language; for example, a simulation of a bank that can be made specific by stating the number of tellers, number of customers, and other parameters.

built-in simulator A simulator that is built in to the system being modeled; for example, an operator training simulator built into the control panel of a power plant, such that the system can operate in simulator mode or in normal operating mode. Also called embedded training.

cancellation A mechanism used in optimistic synchronization mechanisms such as Time Warp to delete a previously scheduled event. Cancellation is a mechanism used within the Time Warp executive and is normally not visible to the federate. It is implemented (in part) using the Runtime Infrastructure's event retraction mechanism.

capability Within the fidelity taxonomy, a property that describes a type of action that a DIS resource can perform or represent. See also *fidelity taxonomy.*

causal order A partial ordering of messages based on the "causally happens before" ($\rightarrow$) relationship. A message delivery service is said to be causally ordered if for any two messages M_1 and M_2 (containing notifications of events E_1 and E_2, respectively) that are delivered to a single federate where $E_1 \rightarrow E_2$, M_1 is delivered to the federate before M_2.

characteristic Within the fidelity taxonomy, a distinctive quality of an implementation. See also *fidelity taxonomy.*

class A description of a group of objects with similar properties, common behavior, common relationships, and common semantics.

class hierarchy A specification of a class-subclass or "is-a" relationship between object classes in a given domain.

CMMS The Conceptual Model of the Mission Space (CMMS) is one of the three components of the Department of Defense technical framework. The CMMS is first an abstraction of the real world and serves as a frame of reference for simulation development by capturing the basic information about important entities involved in any mission and their key actions and interactions. A CMMS is a simulation-neutral view of those entities, actions, and interactions occurring in the real world.

common federation functionality Agreements on common simulation functionality (services and resources) that are finalized among all participants in the federation during the federation development process. During federal development, federation members identified during federation design propose opportunities for common services in areas of assigned responsibilities (also established during federation design) during federation development for discussion and negotiation among all federation participants. For instance, agreements on common representations of terrain (data source, resolution, dynamic vs. static, and so forth) and environment (required types, data sources, resolution, servers, and so forth) would be negotiated and agreed to, as would any relevant federation-specific algorithms (e.g., extrapolation).

common-use Modeling and simulation applications, services, or materials provided by a Department of Defense component to two or more Department of Defense components.

component class An object class that is a component or part of a "composite" object that represents a unified assembly of many different object classes.

Computer Generated Force (CGF) Simulation of friendly, enemy, and neutral entities on the virtual battlefield in which the individual platforms are operated by computer simulation of the crew and command hierarchy. See also *virtual battlefield.*

conceptual analysis The step in the federation development and execution process that establishes the conceptual framework for the federation. It feeds the design of the overall federation structure. The conceptual view of the objects and interactions that must be represented in the federation is key to identifying reuse opportunities in established Federation Object Models (FOMs) and to determine candidates for federation membership. The high-level representation of the federation scenario refined during conceptual analysis also provides the basis for generation of a more detailed scenario instance during federation design and development.

conceptual model A statement of the content and internal representations that are the developers' concept of the model. It includes logic and algorithms and explicitly recognizes assumptions and limitations.

concrete model A model in which at least one component represented is a tangible object; for example, a physical replica of a building.

condition The values assumed at a given instant by the variables in a system, model, or simulation. See also *boundary condition; final condition; initial condition; state.*

conditional event A sequentially dependent event that will occur only if some other event has already taken place. See also *time-dependent event.*

conservative synchronization A mechanism that prevents a federate from processing messages out of time stamp order. This is in contrast to optimistic synchronization. The Chandy/Misra/Bryant null message protocol is an example of a conservative synchronization mechanism.

constrained simulation A simulation in which time advances are paced to have a specific relationship to wall-clock time. These are commonly referred to as real-time or scaled-real-time simulations. Here, the terms constrained simulation and (scaled) real-time simulation are used synonymously. Human-in-the-loop (e.g., training exercises) and hardware-in-the-loop (e.g., test and evaluation simulations) are examples of constrained simulations.

constructive simulation A form of simulation, commonly called war games, that involves software representation of two or more opposing forces, using rules, data, and procedures designed to depict an actual or real-life situation. Also called higher-order model (HOM); continuous-change model. See *continuous model.*

continuous model (1) A mathematical or computational model whose output variables change in a continuous manner. That is, by changing from one value to another, a variable can take on all intermediate values; for example, a model depicting the rate of airflow over an airplane wing. Also called continuous-variable model. (2) A model of a system that behaves in a continuous manner. Contrast with *discrete model.*

continuous simulation A simulation that uses a continuous model.

continuous-variable model See *continuous model.*

control station (1) Facility that provides the individual responsible for controlling the simulation and that provides the capability to implement simulation control as Protocol Data Units (PDUs) on the DIS network.

cooperative development Refers to a project in which two or more Department of Defense components share in domain research, technical studies, or technology development, but the result may be in dissimilar modeling and simulation applications.

coordinated time advancement A time advancement mechanism whereby logical clock advances within each federate occur only after some coordination is performed among the federates participating in the execution (e.g., to ensure that the federate never receives an event notice in its past). The Aggregate Level Simulation Program, for example, uses coordinated time advancement.

correlation metrics The quantifiable common characteristic between different databases (e.g., position, orientation, size, shape, material composition, color, topology, trafficability).

critical event simulation A simulation that is terminated by the occurrence of a certain event; for example, a model depicting the year-by-year forces leading up to a volcanic eruption that is terminated when the volcano in the model erupts. See also *time-slice simulation.*

data Representations of facts, concepts, or instructions in a formalized manner suitable for communication, interpretation, or processing by human or automatic means.

current time (of a federate). Same as *federate time.*

data certification The formal determination that data have satisfied verification and validation criteria, which may vary according to usage (e.g., domain [general] or application specific).

data logger A device that accepts Protocol Data Units (PDUs) from the network and stores them for later replay on the network in the same time sequence as the PDUs were originally received. See also *Protocol Data Unit (PDU).*

data validation The formal review of data by subject-area experts and comparison to known existing data or best-estimate values.

data verification The use of formal techniques and procedures to ensure the accuracy and validity of data standards and business rules derived from process and data modeling. Review of the data models to ensure that they are converted and formatted properly for input into the modeling and simulation concept and logical design. Data reduction and transformation processes should be addressed.

database A collection of data, organized according to a schema to serve one or more applications.

Dead Reckoning The process of extrapolating emulation entity position/

orientation based on the last known position/orientation, velocity, and (sometimes) higher-order derivatives of position versus time and/or other vehicle dynamic characteristics.

deaggregate To create multiple entities from an aggregate entity. Contrast with *aggregate.*

Department of Defense Modeling and Simulation executive agent A Department of Defense component to whom the Undersecretary of Defense for Acquisition has assigned responsibility and delegated authority for the development and maintenance of a specific area of modeling and simulation application, including relevant standards and databases, used by or common to many models and simulations.

dependent variable A variable whose value is dependent on the values of one or more independent variables. Contrast with *independent variable.*

descriptive model A model used to depict the behavior or properties of an existing system or type of system; for example, a scale model or written specification used to convey to potential buyers the physical and performance characteristics of a computer. Also called representational model. Contrast with *prescriptive model.*

descriptor Within the fidelity taxonomy, a measurable feature of one or more characteristics that must include units and method of measure. See also *fidelity taxonomy.*

deterministic Pertaining to a process, model, or variable whose outcome, result, or value does not depend on chance. Contrast with *stochastic.*

deterministic model A model in which the results are determined through known relationships among the states and events, and in which a given input will always produce the same output; for example, a model depicting a known chemical reaction. Contrast with *stochastic model.*

digital simulation (1) A simulation that is designed to be executed on a digital system. (2) A simulation that is designed to be executed on an analog system but that represents a digital system. (3) A simulation of a digital circuit. Contrast with *analog simulation.* See also *hybrid simulation.*

DIS See *Distributed Interactive Simulation (DIS).*

DIS component A generic term for any of a range of modeling and simulation products suitable for incorporation into a DIS, including constructive, virtual, and live simulations. See also *Distributed Interactive Simulation.*

DIS control A mechanism that assists users of DIS. See also *Distributed Interactive Simulation.*

DIS entity A protocol entity that conforms to current Institute of Electrical and Electronic Engineers. See also *protocol entity; simulation entity.*

DIS exercise The enactment of a combat engagement (or other operation) potentially including all battlefield (force-on-force) interactions and related activities, such as logistics and intelligence, using DIS. Can include demonstrations, rehearsals, experiments, training events, and field evaluations.

DIS local area network The communications network created by interconnecting DIS components within a DIS node.

DIS network The simulation communications network created as a result of the connection of multiple DIS nodes during DIS exercises.

DIS network interface library A software library required for an application to interface to the network at the revision level defined by the Protocol Data Unit standard indicated. This is the common building block for all DIS architecture components.

DIS network interface unit The interface between the DIS network and a group of simulators, constructive simulations, or live instrumented equipment.

DIS network manager A specified agency with the responsibility for managing the physical network that connects to the DIS network. Responsibilities include approval/acceptance of DIS participants; scheduling of DIS utilization; and coordinating functional, technical, and user communities network requirements.

DIS node One or more simulators, constructive simulations, or pieces of live instrumented equipment that conform to the DIS standards that are connected to the DIS network.

DIS operational manager Overall coordinator of DIS operations. The person who keeps a current listing of all DIS-compatible simulations; coordinates with the network manager to resolve coordination and scheduling conflicts, as necessary; catalogs, stocks, and issues three-dimensional models, associated operational models, and terrain databases; and coordinates development of required terrain databases. See *DIS network manager.*

DIS resource A combination of hardware and software components that can be connected to and interoperate within a DIS exercise. See also *fidelity taxonomy.*

DIS user Customer requiring DIS resources to address training, testing, operational, or analysis objectives.

discrete change model See *discrete model.*

discrete event model See *discrete model.*

discrete model (1) A mathematical or computational model whose output variables take on only discrete values. That is, in changing from one value to another, they do not take on the intermediate values; for example, a model that predicts an organization's inventory levels based on varying shipments and receipts. Also called discrete change model; discrete event model; discrete variable model. (2) A model of a system that behaves in a discrete manner. Contrast with *continuous model.*

discrete simulation A simulation that uses a discrete model.

discrete variable model See *discrete model.*

Distributed Exercise Management (DEM) The tools and methods used to manage a DIS session. A DIS exercise may be composed of simulation assets deployed across a wide geographical area. Each user brings unique requirements to DIS, and not all users require the same amount of exercise management. DEM offers the user a set of control and management choices that can be exercised optionally.

Distributed Interactive Simulation (DIS) A time- and space-coherent synthetic representation of world environments designed to link the interactive, free-play activities of people in operational exercises. The synthetic environment is created through the real-time exchange of data units between distributed, computationally autonomous simulation applications in the form of simulations, simulators, and instrumented equipment that are interconnected through standard computer communication services. The computational simulation entities may be present in one location or they may be distributed geographically.

dynamic model A model of a system in which there is change, such as the occurrence of events over time or the movement of objects through space; for example, a model of a bridge that is subjected to a moving load to determine characteristics of the bridge under changing stress. Contrast with *static model.*

electromagnetic environment (EME) The observable effect of the power and time distribution in various frequency ranges of the radiated or conducted electromagnetic emission levels that may be encountered by a military force, system, or platform when performing its assigned mission in its intended operational environment. It is the sum of electromagnetic interference; electromagnetic pulse; hazards of electromagnetic radiation to personnel, ordnance, and volatile materials; and natural phenomena effects of lightning and static.

electronic battlefield See *synthetic environment.*

embedded training See *built-in simulation.*

emitter A device that is able to discharge a detectable electromagnetic or acoustic energy.

empirical Pertaining to information that is derived from observation, experiment, or experience.

emulate To represent a system by a model that accepts the same inputs and produces the same outputs as the system represented; for example, to emulate an eight-bit computer with a thirty-two-bit computer. See also *simulate.*

emulation (1) A model that accepts the same inputs and produces the same outputs as a given system. See also *simulation.* (2) The process of developing or using a model as in (1).

emulator A device, computer program, or system that performs emulation.

endogenous variable A variable whose value is determined by conditions and events within a given model. Also called internal variable. Contrast with *exogenous variable.*

entity See *simulation entity.*

entity coordinates Location with respect to a simulation entity.

entity perspective The perception of the synthetic environment held by a simulation entity based on its knowledge of itself and its interactions with the other simulation entities. This includes not only its own view of the simulated physical environment (terrain, air, and sea) but also its own view of itself, the other entities in the synthetic environment, and the effects of the other entities on itself and the synthetic environment. Also called battlefield view; world view.

environment (1) The texture or detail of the domain (e.g., terrain relief, weather, day or night, terrain cultural features [such as cities or farmland], sea states). (2) The external objects, conditions, and processes that influence the behavior of a system.

environmental entity A simulation entity that corresponds to dynamic elements of the state of the geographic, atmospheric, and bathyspheric environment of the synthetic environment that can be seen or sensed on a real battlefield; for example, craters, smoke, building collapse, weather conditions, and sea state. See also *simulation entity.*

environmental server A component responsible for maintaining and disseminating the dynamic information on the state of the natural or man-made environment represented in a session, including such things as cratering, smoke, building collapse, weather conditions, and sea state, regardless of their cause. Also called environmental simulator. See also *environmental simulation.*

environmental simulation A simulation that depicts all or part of the natural or man-made environment of a system. See also *environmental server.*

environmental simulator See *environmental server.*

equilibrium See *steady state.*

equilibrium condition See *final condition.*

error model (1) A model used to estimate or predict the extent of deviation of the behavior of an actual system from the desired behavior of the system; for example, a model of a communications channel, used to estimate the number of transmission errors that can be expected on the channel. (2) In software evaluation, a model used to estimate or predict the number of remaining faults, required test time, and similar characteristics of a system. Also called error prediction model.

error prediction model See *error model.*

Euler angles A set of three angles used to describe the orientation of an entity as three successive rotations about three different orthogonal axes (x, y, and z). The order of rotation is first about z by angle psi, then about the new y by angle theta, then about the newest x by angle phi. Angles psi and phi range between plus and minus pi, whereas angle theta ranges only between plus and minus pi/2 radians. These angles specify the successive rotations needed to transform from the world coordinate system to the entity coordinate system. The positive direction of rotation about an axis is defined by the right-hand rule.

event (1) An occurrence that causes a change of state in a simulation. See also *conditional event; time-dependent event.* (2) The instant in time at which a change in some variable occurs. (3) From the High Level Architecture, a change of object attribute value, an interaction between objects, an instantiation of a new object, or a deletion of an existing object that is associated with a particular point on the federation time axis. Each event contains a time stamp indicating when it is said to occur. See also *message.*

event notice A message containing event information.

event-driven simulation See *event-oriented simulation.*

event-oriented simulation A simulation in which attention is focused on the occurrence of events and the times at which those events occur; for example, a simulation of a digital circuit that focuses on the time of state transition. Also called event-driven simulation; event-sequenced simulation.

event-sequenced simulation See *event-oriented simulation.*

exception An exception in the programming language sense of a possible error, signaling return value. The initiator will be informed of these exceptions.

Executive Council for Modeling and Simulations (EXCIMS) An organization established by the Undersecretary of Defense for Acquisition that is responsible for providing advice and assistance on Department of Defense modeling and simulation issues. Membership is determined by the Undersecretary and is at the senior executive service, flag, and general officer levels.

exercise See *field exercise; simulation exercise.*

exercise controller An individual who assists the exercise manager. See also *exercise manager.*

exercise database (1) A standard DIS database that includes network initialization data and simulation entity initialization and control data. (2) The database that contains the machine-independent information necessary to initiate the simulation entity and simulation asset types into a particular session. Also called session database.

exercise manager The test director or training officer who manages the setup, control, and feedback of a simulation exercise after the computer network is activated. This individual is part of the user organization. Also called simulation manager.

exercise segment A discrete Protocol Data Unit (PDU) segment bounded by save state or ENDEX PDUs. Exercise segments may be linked in series or parallel.

exogenous variable A variable whose value is determined by conditions and events external to a given model. Also called external variable. Contrast with *endogenous variable.*

external variable See *exogenous variable.*

face validation The process of determining whether a model or simulation based on performance seems reasonable to people knowledgeable about the system under study. The process does not review software code or logic but rather reviews the inputs and outputs to ensure that they appear realistic or representative.

fast time (1) Simulated time that represents more than a given period of actual time in the system being modeled. For example, in a simulation of plant growth, running the simulation for one second may result in the model advancing time by one full day; that is, simulated time advances faster than actual time. (2) The duration of activities within a simulation in which simulated time advances faster than actual time. Contrast with *real time; slow time.*

feature A static element of the synthetic environment that exists but does not actively participate in synthetic environment interactions. Features are represented in the implementation environment by cartographic databases that are used by simulation assets. Entities can interact with features (building them, destroying them, colliding with them, and so forth), but features are passive in that they do not initiate action. When features are dynamic (e.g., dynamic terrain) they are called environmental entities. See also *environmental entity; synthetic environment.*

federate A member of a High Level Architecture Federation. All applications participating in a federation are called federates. In reality, this may include federate managers, data collectors, live entity surrogates, simulations, or passive viewers.

federate time Scaled wall-clock time or logical time of a federate, whichever is smaller. Federate time is synonymous with the current time of the federate. At any instant of an execution different federates will, in general, have different federate times.

federation A named set of interacting federates, a common federation object model, and a supporting Runtime Infrastructure that are used as a whole to achieve some specific objective.

federation execution The federation execution represents the actual operation, over time, of a subset of the federates and the Runtime Infrastructure initialization data taken from a particular federation. It is the step in which the executable code is run to conduct the exercise and produce the data for the measures of effectiveness for the federation execution.

federation execution sponsor Federation development begins with a user and a requirement. The federation execution sponsor is the organization that uses the results and/or products from a specific application of modeling and simulation. It is the group responsible for establishing the need for the development and execution of a federation. It also establishes the framework for the measures of effectiveness by which the results of the execution are employed.

Federation Object Model (FOM) An identification of the essential classes of objects, object attributes, and object interactions that are supported by a High Level Architecture federation. Optional classes of additional information may also be specified to achieve a more complete description of the federation structure and/or behavior.

federation objectives The statement of the problem that is to be addressed by the establishment and execution of a federation. The description of the problem domain implicit in the objectives statement is critical for focusing the domain analysis activities in the conceptual analysis phase. It specifies the top-level goals of the federation and may specify the operational need or shortfall from which federation developers will derive a scenario for the federation execution. The federation objectives drive this specification, as the scenario development phase must utilize the statement of objectives to generate a viable context for system evaluations intrinsic to the federation objectives. High-level testing requirements implied in the federation objectives may also drive the identification of well-defined "test points" during development of the federation scenario.

federation time axis A totally ordered sequence of values in which each value represents an instant of time in the physical system being modeled, and for any two points T_1 and T_2 on the federation time axis, if $T_1 < T_2$, then T_1 represents an instant of physical time that occurs before the instant represented by T_2. Logical time, scaled wall-clock time, and federate time specify points on the federation time axis. The progression of a federate along the federation time axis during an execution may or may not have a direct relationship to the progression of wall-clock time.

fidelity (1) The similarity, both physical and functional, between the simulation and that which it simulates. (2) A measure of the realism of a simulation. (3) The degree of similarity between a model and the system properties being modeled. Also called correspondence. See also *model validation*.

fidelity domain Resource that may affect the fidelity of a DIS exercise (examples are battlespace entities, environments, hosts, and sites). See also *fidelity taxonomy*.

fidelity management A process to level the playing field by dynamically varying fidelity parameters of dissimilar simulators.

fidelity taxonomy The systematic categorization of simulations into groupings of common levels of physical and modeling characteristics.

field A series of contiguous bits treated as an instance of a particular data type that may be part of a higher-level data structure.

field exercise An exercise conducted in the field under simulated war conditions in which troops and armament of one side are actually present, and those of the other side may be imaginary or in outline. See also *simulation exercise*.

filtering Accepting or rejecting Protocol Data Units received on the network based on specified criteria, which may be dynamically varied. Examples include geographical filtering and entity-type filtering.

final condition The values assumed by the variables in a system, model, or simulation at the completion of some specified duration of time. Also called equilibrium condition. Contrast with *boundary condition; initial condition.*

final state The values assumed by the state variables of a system, component, or simulation at the completion of some specified duration of time. Contrast with *initial state.*

FRED The Federation Required Execution Details (FRED) are global specifications of several classes of information needed by the Runtime Infrastructure to instantiate an execution of the federation. Additional execution-specific information needed to fully establish the "contract" between federation members (e.g., publish responsibilities or subscription requirements) is also documented in the FRED. The set of management requirements provides one source of input to the FRED specification, which is recorded in a standardized format.

game A physical or mental competition in which the participants, called players, seek to achieve some objective within a given set of rules. See also *game theory.*

game theory (1) The study of situations involving competing interests, modeled in terms of the strategies, probabilities, actions, gains, and losses of opposing players in a game. See also *management game; war game.* (2) The study of games to determine the probability of winning, given various strategies.

gaming simulation See *simulation game.*

general-use modeling and simulation applications Specific representations of the physical environment or environmental effects used by, or common to, many models and simulations (e.g., terrain, atmospheric, or hydrographic effects).

glass box model A model whose internal implementation is known and fully visible; for example, a model of a computerized change-return mechanism in a vending machine, in the form of a diagram of the circuits and gears that make the change. Also called white box model. Contrast with *black box model.*

granularity See *resolution.*

graphic model A symbolic model whose properties are expressed in diagrams; for example, a decision tree used to express a complex procedure. Contrast with *mathematical model; narrative model; software model; tabular model.*

Greenwich Mean Time (GMT) Mean solar time for the Greenwich meridian, counted from midnight through twenty-four hours. Also called universal time coordinated (UTC) or Zulu time.

guise A function that provides the capability for an entity to be viewed with one appearance by one group of participants, and with another appearance by another group.

happens before, causal ($\rightarrow$) A relationship between two actions A_1 and A_2 (where an action can be an event, a Runtime Infrastructure [RTI] message send, or an RTI message receive) defined as follows: if A_1 and A_2 occur in the same federate/RTI, and A_1 precedes A_2 in that federate/RTI, then $A_1 \rightarrow A_2$; if A_1 is a message send action and A_2 is a receive action for the same message, then $A_1 \rightarrow A_2$; if $A_1 \rightarrow A_2$ and if $A_1 \rightarrow A_2$ and $A_2 \rightarrow A_3$, then $A_1 \rightarrow A_3$ (transitivity).

happens before, temporal ($\rightarrow_t$) A relationship between two events E_1 and E_2 defined as follows: if E_1 has a smaller time stamp than E_2, then $E_1 \rightarrow_t E_2$. The Runtime Infrastructure provides an internal tie-breaking mechanism to ensure (in effect) that no two events observed by a single federate contain the same time stamp.

heterogeneous network A network of DIS objects with partially consistent behaviors and/or partially correlated databases. Examples of heterogeneous networks are networks of simulators of varying fidelity, networks of simulators and actual equipment operating on instrumented ranges, and mixes of simulators and aggregated (unit-level) simulations.

heuristic Pertaining to experimental, especially trial-and-error, methods of problem solving. *Note:* The resulting solution may not be the most desirable solution to the problem.

higher-order model (HOM) A computer model representing combat elements, their functions, and/or the terrain they operate on in an aggregated manner. An HOM may represent a battalion as a specific entity that is a conglomeration or averaging of the characteristics of its real-world components. "Higher order" generally refers to echelons of battalion and above with coarser than 100 m resolution (e.g., 3 km) and with faster than real-time performance (e.g., days compressed into minutes, hours into seconds). Also called war game; constructive simulation.

homogeneous network A network of DIS objects with fully consistent behaviors and fully correlated databases.

host computer A computer that supports one or more simulation applications. All host computers participating in a simulation exercise are connected by a common network.

human-machine simulation A simulation carried out by both human participants and computers, typically with the human participants asked to make decisions and a computer performing processing based on those decisions; for example, a simulation in which humans make automotive design decisions and a computer determines and displays the results of those decisions.

hybrid simulation A simulation, in which some portions are designed to be executed on an analog system and other portions on a digital system.

Interaction between the two portions may take place during execution. See also *analog simulation; digital simulation.*

iconic model A physical model or graphic display that looks like the system being modeled; for example, a nonfunctional replica of a computer tape drive used for display purposes. See also *scale model.*

identity simulation A simulation in which the roles of the participants are investigated or defined; for example, a simulation that identifies aircraft based on their physical profiles, speed, altitude, and acoustic characteristics.

implementation (1) The means by which a synthetic environment or portions of a synthetic environment are realized. (2) Within the fidelity taxonomy, the means by which a capability is realized. See also *fidelity taxonomy.*

Implementation environment The details and mechanics of the underlying networked simulation system that generates the synthetic environment. The implementation environment includes both the simulation assets and the supporting networks. Also called physical realization.

in-basket simulation A simulation in which a set of issues is presented to a participant in the form of documents on which action must be taken; for example, a simulation of an unfolding international crisis as a sequence of memos describing relevant events and outcomes of the participant's actions on previous memos.

independent time advancement A means of advancing federate time in which advances occur without explicit coordination among federates. DIS is an example of a federation using independent time advancement.

independent variable A variable whose value is not dependent on the values of other variables. Contrast with *dependent variable.*

independent verification and validation The conduct of verification and validation of a model or simulation by individuals or agencies that did not develop the model or simulation.

initial condition The values assumed by the variables in a system, model, or simulation at the beginning of some specified duration of time. Contrast with *boundary condition; final condition.*

initial state The values assumed by the state variables of a system, component, or simulation at the beginning of some specified duration of time. Contrast with *final state.*

input/output model See *black box model.*

instructional simulation A simulation intended to provide a simulation equivalent of a real or hypothesized stimulus that could occur in the warfare environment. This can include conveying orders, being in a specific place, firing a weapon, running into a tree, or throwing a track.

interaction An explicit action taken by an object that can optionally (within the bounds of the federation object model) be directed toward other objects, including geographic areas.

interaction parameters The information associated with an interaction that objects potentially affected by the interaction must receive in order to calculate the effects of that interaction on their current state.

interactive model A model that requires human participation. Also called human-in-the-loop model.

intercell database The data needed by cell interface units and cell adapter units to support interoperation of cells.

internal variable See *endogenous variable.*

interoperability The ability of a set of simulation entities to interact with an acceptable degree of fidelity. The acceptability of a model is determined by the user for the specific purpose of the exercise, test, or analysis.

interval-oriented simulation A continuous simulation in which simulated time is advanced in increments of a size suitable to make implementation possible on a digital system.

joint modeling and simulation Abstract representations of joint and service forces, capabilities, equipment, material, and services used in the joint environment or by two or more military Services.

known object An object is known to a federate if the federate is reflecting or updating any attributes of that object.

laboratory simulation A simulation developed and used under highly controlled conditions; for example, a simulation of a medical technique implemented in the controlled environment of a laboratory.

lag variable (1) In a discrete simulation, a variable that is an output of one period and an input for some future period. (2) In an analog simulation, a variable that is a function of an output variable and is used as input to the simulation to provide a time-delay response or feedback. Also called lagged variable; serially-correlated variable.

lagged variable See *lag variable.*

LBTS Lower bound on the time stamp of the next time stamp ordered (TSO) message to be received by a Runtime Infrastructure (RTI) from another federate. Messages with a time stamp less than LBTS are eligible for delivery by the RTI to the federate without compromising TSO delivery guarantees. TSO messages with a time stamp greater than LBTS are not yet eligible for delivery. LBTS is maintained within the RTI using a conservative synchronization protocol.

lead variable (1) In a discrete simulation, a variable that is an output of one period and predicts what the output of some future period will be. (2) In an analog simulation, a variable that is a function of an output variable and is used as input to the simulation to provide advanced-time response or feedback.

live simulation A representation of military operations using military personnel and equipment that simulates experiences achieved during actual combat conditions. Typical live simulations are operational testing, field exercises, training exercises, and force-on-force exercises.

local-area network (LAN) A class of data network that provides high data rate interconnection between network nodes in close physical proximity. LANs are defined by the IEEE 802.X series of standards.

local time The mean solar time for the meridian of the observer.

logical time A federate's current point on the logical time axis. If the federate's logical time is T, all time stamp ordered (TSO) messages with a time stamp less than T have been delivered to the federate, and no TSO messages with a time stamp greater than T have been delivered; some, though not necessarily all, TSO messages with a time stamp equal to T may also have been delivered. Logical time does not, in general, bear a direct relationship to wall-clock time, and advances in logical time are controlled entirely by the federates and the Runtime Infrastructure (RTI). Specifically, the federate requests advances in logical time via the time advance request and next event request RTI services, and the RTI notifies the federate when it has advanced logical time explicitly through the time advance grant service or implicitly by the time stamp of TSO messages that are delivered to the federate. Logical time (along with scaled wall-clock time) is used to determine the current time of the federate (see *federate time*). Logical time is relevant only to federates using TSO message delivery and coordinated time advances and may be ignored (by requesting a time advance to infinity at the beginning of the execution) by other federates.

logical time axis A set of points (instants) on the federation time axis used to specify before and after relationships among events.

long-haul network (LHN) See *wide-area network (WAN)*.

lookahead A value used to determine the smallest time stamped message using the time stamp ordered service that a federate may generate in the future. If a federate's current time (i.e., federate time) is T and its lookahead is L, any message generated by the federate must have a time stamp of at least T + L. In general, lookahead may be associated with an entire federate (as in the example just described, or at a finer level of detail (e.g., from one federate to another or for a specific attribute). Any federate using the time stamp ordered message delivery service must specify a lookahead value.

machine simulation A simulation that is executed on a machine.

man-machine simulation See *human-machine simulation*.

management game A simulation game in which participants seek to achieve a specified management objective, given preestablished resources and constraints; for example, a simulation in which participants make decisions designed to maximize profit in a given business situation and a computer determines the results of those decisions. See also *war game*.

manned platform entity Corresponds to actual battlefield entities or proposed battlefield entities that are driven, guided, flown, or otherwise have a warfighter, staff, or crew in the loop. This includes command posts and other command, control, communication, and intelligence (C3I) nodes and may include role-players representing other battlefield entities or staff functions.

Markov chain model A discrete, stochastic model in which the probability that the model is in a given state at a certain time depends only on the value of the immediately preceding state. Also called Markov model. See also *semi-Markov model.*

Markov model See *Markov chain model.*

Markov process A stochastic process that assumes that in a series of random events, the probability for the occurrence of each event depends only on the immediately preceding outcome. See also *semi-Markov process.*

mathematical model A symbolic model whose properties are expressed in mathematical symbols and relationships; for example, a model of a nation's economy expressed as a set of equations. Contrast with *graphic model; narrative model; software model; tabular model.*

mean solar time A measurement of time using the diurnal motion of a fictitious body (called the "mean sun") that is supposed to move uniformly in the celestial equator, completing the circuit in one tropical year. Often termed simply mean time. The mean sun may be considered as moving in the celestial equator and having a right ascension equal to the mean celestial longitude of the true sun. At any given instant, mean solar time is the hour angle of the mean sun. In civil life, mean solar time is counted from the two branches of the meridian through twelve hours; the hours from the lower branch are marked A.M. (antemeridian), and those from the upper branch, P.M. (postmeridian). In astronomical work, mean solar time is counted from the lower branch of the meridian through twenty-four hours. Naming the meridian of reference is essential to the complete identification of time. The Greenwich meridian is the reference for a worldwide standard of mean solar time called Greenwich Mean Time (GMT) or Universal Time Coordinated (UTC).

measure of performance (MOP) Measure of how the system or individual performs its functions in a given environment (e.g., probability of detection, reaction time, number of targets nominated, susceptibility of deception, task completion time). It is closely related to inherent parameters (physical and structural) but measures attributes of system behavior.

message A data unit transmitted between federates containing at most one event. Here, a message typically contains information concerning an event and is used to notify another federate that the event has occurred. When it contains such event information, the message's time stamp is defined as the time stamp of the event to which it corresponds. Here, a message corresponds to a single event, but the physical transport media may include several such messages in a single physical message that is transmitted through the network.

message (event) delivery Invocation of the corresponding service (reflect attribute values, receive interaction, instantiate discovered object, or remove object) by the Runtime Infrastructure (RTI) to notify a federate of the occurrence of an event.

military departments The Department of the Army, the Department of the Navy, and the Department of the Air Force, including their National Guard and Reserve components.

military services The U.S. Army, Navy, Air Force, and Marine Corps.

mission planning system A component that provides mission planning equipment capabilities on the DIS local-area network.

mock-up A full-sized structural, but not necessarily functional, model built accurately to scale, used chiefly for study, testing, or display; for example, a full-sized model of an airplane displayed in a museum. See also *physical model*.

model A physical, mathematical, or otherwise logical representation of a system, entity, phenomenon, or process. (1) An approximation, representation, or idealization of selected aspects of the structure, behavior, operation, or other characteristics of a real-world process, concept, or system. *Note:* Models may have other models as components. (2) To serve as a model as in (1). (3) To develop or use a model as in (1). (4) A mathematical or otherwise logical representation of a system or a system's behavior over time.

model provider Organization that develops and maintains entity or environment models for use in DIS exercises.

model validation The process of determining the degree to which the requirements, design, or implementation of a model is a realization of selected aspects of the system being modeled. See also *fidelity*. Contrast with *model verification*.

model verification The process of determining the degree of similarity between the realization steps of a model; for example, between the requirements and the design, or between the design and its implementation. Contrast with *model validation*.

modeling and simulation interoperability The ability of a model or simulation to provide services to, and accept services from, other models and simulations, and to use the services so exchanged to enable them to operate effectively together.

modeling and simulation investment plan A Department of Defense plan, published under the authority of the Undersecretary of Defense for Acquisition and with the coordination of the Department of Defense components, that establishes short-term (present to six years) and long-term (beyond six years) programs and funding for joint- and common- use modeling and simulation to achieve the specified goals and objectives outlined in the Department of Defense modeling and simulation master plan.

modeling and simulation master plan A Department of Defense plan, published under the authority of the Undersecretary of Defense for Acquisition and with the coordination of the Department of Defense components, that establishes short-term (present to six years) and long-term (beyond six years) Department of Defense goals and objectives for the application of modeling and simulation for joint and common use within the Department of Defense. It also includes an assessment of current modeling and simulation capabilities, a status report on modeling and simulation efforts under development, and a road map that delineates the management, investment, and technical strategies required to achieve Department of Defense modeling and simulation objectives.

Monte Carlo method In modeling and simulation, any method that employs Monte Carlo simulation to determine estimates for unknown values in a deterministic problem. See also *stochastic model.*

Monte Carlo simulation A simulation in which random statistical sampling techniques are employed, such that the result determines estimates for unknown values.

multicast A transmission mode in which a single message is sent to multiple network destinations (i.e., one to many).

narrative model A symbolic model whose properties are expressed in words; for example, a written specification for a computer system. Also called verbal-descriptive model. Contrast with *graphic model; mathematical model; software model; tabular model.*

natural model A model that represents a system by another system that already exists in the real world; for example, a model that uses one body of water to represent another.

network filter A system of network addresses to selectively accept or reject Protocol Data Units received from the network.

network management The collection of administrative structures, policies, and procedures that provide for the management of the organization and operation of the network as a whole. See also network manager.

network manager The person responsible for maintaining, monitoring, and scheduling the operation of the DIS network whose responsibilities for the network terminate at the gateways (whether inside or outside the gateway depends on which gateway is in use). Normally, the individual is also in charge of the gateway and is not part of the user organization. See also *network management.*

network node A specific network address. See also *node.*

network scheduler The person responsible for scheduling all use of the DIS network. This includes use for video teleconferencing and simulation. Duties include maintaining and distributing the schedule, coordinating users, assigning unique exercise IDs, ascertaining network loading demands, and resolving conflicts.

network theory The study of networks used to model processes such as communications, computer performance, routing problems, and project management.

nodalization (1) The set of nodes within a system being modeled. (2) The process of developing the nodes as in (1).

node (1) A single entity that is represented in a mathematical model; for example, in a model of a nuclear reactor, a water pump or section of pipe. (2) A general term denoting either a switching element in a network or a host computer attached to a network. See also *DIS node; network node; processing node.*

nonabsorbing state In a Markov chain model, a state that can be left once it is entered. Contrast with *absorbing state.*

non-standard cell A cell that is not compliant with the DIS message and database standards. Nonstandard cells require a cell adapter unit in order to join a DIS exercise.

normative model A model that makes use of a familiar situation to represent a less familiar one; for example, a model that depicts the human cardiovascular system by using a mechanical pump, rubber hoses, and water.

numerical model (1) A mathematical model in which a set of mathematical operations is reduced to a form suitable for solution by a simpler method such as numerical analysis or automation; for example, a model in which a single equation representing a nation's economy is replaced by a large set of simple averages based on empirical observations of inflation rate, unemployment rate, gross national product, and other indicators. (2) A model whose properties are expressed by numbers.

object A fundamental element of a conceptual representation for a federate that reflects the real world at levels of abstraction and resolution appropriate for federate interoperability. For any given value of time, the state of an object is defined as the enumeration of all its attribute values.

object based A software design methodology adhering to only some of the properties of object-oriented software; for example, because Ada does not support inheritance, a key property of object-oriented systems, it is often referred to as an object-based language. See also *object oriented.*

object model A specification of the objects intrinsic to a given system, including a description of the object characteristics (attributes) and a description of the static and dynamic relationships that exist between objects.

object model framework The rules and terminology used to describe High Level Architecture object models.

object oriented A software design methodology that (when applied to DIS) results in a battlefield that is represented by objects that encapsulate associated methods or procedures and where objects communicate by message passing. Examples of battlefield objects are platoons (unit level), tanks (platform level), main guns (component or module level), and gun barrels (part level). Object-oriented designs have inherent modularity (e.g., to change a tank model, only the tank object must be changed). See also *object based.*

object ownership Ownership of the ID attribute of an object, initially established by use of the instantiate object interface service. Encompasses the privilege of deleting the object using the Delete Object service. Can be transferred to another federate using the attribute ownership management services.

Office of the Secretary of Defense (OSD) Includes the immediate offices of the Secretary and Deputy Secretary of Defense, the Undersecretaries of Defense, the Comptroller of the Department of Defense, the Director of Defense Research and Engineering, the Assistant Secretaries of Defense, the general counsel of the Department of Defense, the Assistants to the Secretary of Defense, the OSD directors or equivalents who report directly to the Secretary or the Deputy Secretary of Defense, and such other staff offices as the Secretary of Defense establishes to assist in carrying out assigned responsibilities.

open systems environment A DIS environment having attributes of interoperability and portability that promotes competition by allowing systems developed by multiple vendors and nations to interoperate through a common set of computer and communications protocols. Also called open systems interconnection (OSI).

open systems interconnection (OSI) See *open systems environment.*

operational environment A composite of the conditions, circumstances, and influences that affect the employment of military forces and the decisions of the unit commander. Frequently characterized as permissive, semipermissive, or nonpermissive.

optimistic synchronization A mechanism that uses a recovery mechanism to erase the effects of out-of-order event processing. This is in contrast to conservative synchronization. The Time Warp protocol is an example of an optimistic synchronization mechanism. Messages sent by an optimistic federate that could later be canceled are referred to as optimistic messages.

outcome-oriented simulation A simulation in which the end result is considered more important than the process by which it is obtained; for example, a simulation of a radar system that uses methods far different from those used by the actual radar, but whose output is the same. Contrast with *process-oriented simulation.*

own entity approximation An extrapolation of the state vector of the own entity based on last known data.

owned attribute An object attribute that is explicitly modeled by the owning federate. A federate that owns an attribute has the unique responsibility to provide values for that attribute to the federation, through the Runtime Infrastructure, as they are produced.

PDU See *Protocol Data Unit.*

period The time interval between successive events in a discrete simulation.

Petri net An abstract, formal model of information flow, showing static and dynamic properties of a system.

physical model A model whose physical characteristics resemble the physical characteristics of the system being modeled; for example, a plastic or wooden replica of an airplane. Contrast with *symbolic model.* See also *iconic model; mock-up; scale model.*

physical realization The details and mechanics of the underlying networked simulation system that generates the illusion of the virtual battlefield. Includes both the simulation nodes and the supporting networks. Also called implementation environment.

plan view display A symbolic representation of a DIS exercise in which the observer's eye point is above the exercise.

platform A generic term used to describe a level of representation equating to vehicles, aircraft, missiles, ships, fixed sites, and so forth in the hierarchy of representation possibilities. Other representation levels include units (made up of platforms) and components or modules (which make up platforms).

predictive model A model in which the values of future states can be predicted or are hypothesized; for example, a model that predicts weather patterns based on the current value of temperature, humidity, wind speed, and so on at various locations.

prescriptive model A model used to convey the required behavior or properties of a proposed system; for example, a scale model or written specification used to convey to a computer supplier the physical and performance characteristics of a required computer. Contrast with *descriptive model.*

principal staff assistants The Undersecretaries of Defense; the Comptroller; the assistant secretaries; the Inspector General of the Department of Defense; the general counsel; the Assistants to the Secretary of Defense; and the directors or equivalents who report directly to the Secretary or Deputy Secretary of Defense.

probabilistic model See *stochastic model.*

process model A model of the processes performed by a system; for example, a model that represents the software development process as a sequence of phases. Contrast with *structural model.*

process-oriented simulation A simulation in which the process is considered more important than the outcome; for example, a model of a radar system in which the objective is to replicate exactly the radar's operation, and duplication of its results is a lesser concern. Contrast with *outcome-oriented simulation.*

processing node The hardware and software processing resources devoted to one or more simulation entities. See also *node.*

protocol A set of rules and formats (semantic and syntactic) that define the communication behavior of simulation applications.

protocol catalog Envisioned as an on-line database that will contain standard definitions and formats of data exchanged between distributed simulations. This will help achieve a particular "collective" functionality distributed among multiple federates (e.g., air defense, logistics, anti-submarine warfare, and so forth). During federation design, this repository is accessed (via automated browsing tools) to identify individual interactions for which a federate will be required, thus helping to define the federation design. The database will be accessible via the World Wide Web. Copies of the protocol catalog can be made and extended by government agencies as necessary to cover classified data. An official unclassified copy will be maintained by the DIS standards workshop.

Protocol Data Unit (PDU) A structured message that transfers essential data of a specific type from one DIS entity to another and allows them to participate in a common exercise.

Protocol Data Unit decoder A device that decodes Protocol Data Units (PDUs) located in the input buffer using the PDU standard revision level indicated. See also *Protocol Data Unit (PDU)*.

Protocol Data Unit generator Generates Protocol Data Units (PDUs) using the PDU standard revision level and stores them in the output buffer. See also *Protocol Data Unit (PDU)*.

Protocol Data Unit translation Process that translates DIS Protocol Data Units (PDUs) at the revision level indicated to and from SIMNET PDUs. See also *Protocol Data Unit (PDU)*.

protocol entity An object that exchanges information with other protocol entities in a network via Protocol Data Units (PDUs) in accordance with an established protocol. A key attribute of a protocol entity is its state. State transitions occur in a given protocol entity in accordance with the established protocol as the result of (1) PDUs received from other protocol entities, and (2) the occurrence of an external event (e.g., expiration of a time-out counter). See also *Protocol Data Unit (PDU)*.

prototype A preliminary type, form, or instance of a system that serves as a model for later stages or for the final, complete version of the system.

queue In queuing theory, a set of zero or more entities waiting to be serviced by a service facility.

queuing model A model consisting of service facilities and entities waiting in queues to be served; for example, a model depicting teller windows and customers at a bank.

queuing network model A model in which a process is described as a network in which each node represents a service facility rendering a given type of service and a queue for holding entities waiting to be served; for example, a model depicting a network of shipping routes and docking facilities at which ships must form queues in order to unload their cargo.

queuing theory The study of queues and of the performance of systems that service entities that are organized into queues. See also *queuing model; queuing network model*.

random Pertaining to a process or variable whose outcome or value depends on chance or on a process that simulates chance, often with the implication that all possible outcomes or values have an equal probability of occurrence; for example, the outcome of flipping a coin or executing a computer-programmed random number generator.

real battlefield See *real world*.

real time (1) In modeling and simulation, simulated time that represents a given period of actual time in the system being modeled. For example, in a simulation of a radar system, running the simulation for one second may result in the model advancing time by one second; that is, simulated time advances at the same rate as actual time. Contrast with *fast time; slow time*. (2) Refers to an event or data transfer in which, unless accomplished within an allotted amount of time, the accomplishment of the action has either no value or diminishing value. (3) From the High Level Architecture, the actual time in which a physical process occurs.

real-time simulation See *constrained simulation*.

real world The set of real or hypothetical causes and effects that simulation technology attempts to replicate. When used in a military context, the term is synonymous with real battlefield to include air, land, and sea combat.

real-world time The actual time in Greenwich, England. Also called standard Greenwich Mean Time.

receive Transference of a Protocol Data Unit from the DIS network to the input buffer.

reference version The most recent version of a model or simulation that has been released by and is under the configuration management of an approving authority.

reflected attribute An object attribute that is represented but not explicitly modeled in a federate. The reflecting federate accepts new values of the reflected attribute as they are produced by some other federation member and provided by the Runtime Infrastructure.

registration Alignment of coordinate systems and phenomenological agreement between environmental models.

reliability model A model used to estimate, measure, or predict the reliability of a system; for example, a model of a computer system, used to estimate the total downtime that will be experienced.

reliable service A communication service in which the number and type of errors that the user finds in the data are acceptable for the application. Reliable communication may require specific mechanisms in order to achieve the user's requirements: error detection and notification, such as bit errors based on a too-high bit error rate as defined by the user; or error detection and correction from Protocol Data Units (PDU) errors, such as bit errors, duplicated PDUs, missing PDUs, or out-of-sequence PDUs.

remote entity approximation (REA) A general term used to describe the process of extrapolating and interpolating any state of an entity based on its last known state. This includes Dead Reckoning and smoothing. See also *Dead Reckoning*.

representational model See *descriptive model*.

resolution (1) The degree to which near-equal-results values can be discriminated. (2) The measure of the ability to delineate picture detail.

retraction An action performed by a federate to unschedule a previously scheduled event. Event retraction is visible to the federate. Unlike "cancellation," which is relevant only to optimistic federates such as Time Warp, "retraction" is a facility provided to the federate. Retraction is widely used in classic event-oriented discrete event simulations to model behaviors such as preemption and interrupts.

review database (RDB) A database that contains a record of the results of the DIS exercise for later review and analysis.

right-hand rule Positive rotation is clockwise when viewed toward the positive direction along the axis of rotation.

rotational transformation Transformation of a world coordinate system representation or orientation to or from another representation. See also *world coordinate system*.

RTI initialization data (RID) The data required by the Runtime Infrastructure for operation. The required data come from two distinct sources, the Federation Object Model (FOM) product and the Federation Required Execution Details (FRED).

Runtime Infrastructure (RTI) The general-purpose distributed operating system software that provides common interface services during the runtime of a High Level Architecture federation.

scalability The propensity for increasing capability in numbers and complexity of interconnected simulations with the attendant exponentially growing communication requirements.

scale model A physical model that resembles a given system, with only a change in scale; for example, a replica of an airplane one-tenth the size of the actual airplane.

scaled wall-clock time A quantity derived from a wall-clock time defined as offset + [rate $\times$ (wall-clock time – time of last exercise start or restart)]. All scaled wall-clock time values represent points on the federation time axis. If the "rate" factor is k, scaled wall-clock time advances at a rate that is k times faster than wall-clock time.

scenario (1) Description of an exercise ("initial conditions" in military terms). It is part of the session database that configures the units and platforms and places them in specific locations with specific missions. (2) An initial set of conditions and a time line of significant events imposed on trainees or systems to achieve exercise objectives. See also *field exercise*.

scenario development In this phase, the federation developers formulate a scenario whose execution and subsequent evaluation will lead toward achieving the study objectives set forth by the federation sponsor. The scenario provides an identification of the major entities that must be represented by the federation; a conceptual description of the capabilities, behavior, and relationships (interactions) between these major entities over time; and a specification of relevant environmental conditions (e.g., terrain, atmospherics). Initial and termination conditions are also provided. The style and format of the scenario documentation (e.g., graphics, tables, text) are entirely at the discretion of the federation developer. However, communities of users may wish to establish scenario documentation standards among themselves to facilitate reuse of scenario components. The output of this phase is a functional-level scenario description, which is provided as input to the conceptual analysis phase. Certain key activities during conceptual analysis may also drive reiterations of the scenario development phase.

scheduling an event Invocation of a primitive (update attribute values, send interaction, instantiate object, or delete object) by a federate to notify the Runtime Infrastructure (RTI) of the occurrence of an event. Scheduling an event normally results in the RTI sending messages to other federates to notify them of the occurrence of the event. See also *exercise.*

semi-automated forces (SAFOR) See *computer-generated forces (CGF).*

semi-Markov model A Markov chain model in which the length of time spent in each state is randomly distributed.

semi-Markov process A Markov process in which the duration of each event is randomly distributed.

serially correlated variable See *lag variable.*

session The interaction of simulation entities in a synthetic environment generated by simulation assets. Also called exercise.

session database See *exercise database.*

session manager See *exercise manager.*

SI The official abbreviation for Le Systeme International d'Unites, a universal system of metric weights and measures adopted in 1960 by the international authority on the metric system, the Conference Generale des Poids et Measures (CGPM).

SIMNET (simulator network) A Defense Advanced Research Projects Agency (DARPA) project whose goal has been to develop the technology to build a large-scale network of interactive combat simulators.

Simuland The system being simulated by a simulation.

simulate To represent a system by a model that behaves or operates like the system. See also *emulate.*

simulated time Time as represented within a simulation. Also called virtual time. See also *fast time; real time; slow time.*

simulation A method for implementing a model over time. Also, a technique for testing, analysis, or training in which real-world systems are used or in which real-world and conceptual systems are reproduced by a model. (l) A model that behaves or operates like a given system when provided with a set of controlled inputs. Also called simulation model. See also *emulation*. (2) The process of developing or using a model as in (1). (3) Implementation of a special kind of model that represents at least some key internal elements of a system and describes how those elements interact over time. Most combat simulations are implemented as computer programs.

simulation application (1) The executing software on a host computer that generates one or more simulation entities. Examples include manned vehicle simulators, computer-generated forces, and computer interfaces between a DIS network and real equipment. The simulation application receives and processes information concerning entities created by peer simulation applications through the exchange of DIS PDUs. More than one simulation application may simultaneously execute on a host computer. (2) The application layer protocol entity that implements standard DIS protocol. Also called simulation. See also *computer-generated force (CGF)*.

simulation asset Resources used to support the generation of simulation entities within the synthetic environment (e.g., computer, software, human operator, or operational system).

simulation clock A counter used to accumulate simulated time.

simulation database See *exercise database*.

simulation entity An element of the synthetic environment that is created and controlled by a simulation application through the exchange of DIS Protocol Data Units (PDUs) (e.g., tanks, submarines, carriers, fighter aircraft, missiles, bridges). It is possible that a simulation application may be controlling more than one simulation entity. Also called entity.

simulation environment (1) Consists of the operational environment surrounding the simulation entities including terrain, atmospheric, bathyspheric, and cultural information that is adequately correlated for the type of exercise to be performed. (2) All the conditions, circumstances, and influences surrounding and affecting simulation entities, including those stated in (1).

simulation exercise (1) Consists of one or more interacting simulation applications. Simulations participating in the same simulation exercise share a common identifying number called the exercise identifier. These simulations also utilize correlated representations of the synthetic environment in which they operate. (2) The conduct of a session involving one or more cells over a period of time. The term usually has a training connotation and is equivalent to "test," "experiment," or "study scenario." See also *field exercise*.

simulation fidelity Refers to the degree of similarity between the training situation and the operational situation that is being simulated. See also *fidelity taxonomy*.

simulation game A simulation in which the participants seek to achieve some agreed-upon objective within an established set of rules; for example, a management game, a war game. *Note:* The objective may not be to compete but to evaluate the participants, increase their knowledge concerning the simulated scenario, or achieve other goals. Also called gaming simulation.

simulation language A programming language used to implement simulations.

simulation management A mechanism that provides centralized control of the simulation exercise. Functions of simulation management include start, restart, maintenance, shutdown of the exercise, and collection and distribution of certain types of data. See also *exercise.*

simulation manager See *exercise manager.*

simulation model See *simulation.*

Simulation Object Model (SOM) A specification of the intrinsic capabilities that an individual simulation offers to federations. The standard format in which SOMs are expressed provides a means for federation developers to quickly determine the suitability of simulation systems to assume specific roles within a federation.

simulation process The imitative representation of the actions of platforms, munitions, and life forms by computer programs in accordance with a mathematical model and the generation of associated battlefield entities. May be fully or partially automated. In the latter case, the human in the loop injects command-level decisions into the process and is not intended to be a "trainee."

simulation support entity Processing modules used to support, control, or monitor the simulation environment but that do not actually exist on the battlefield. This includes battlefield viewing devices for controllers or exercise observers, such as the stealth vehicle, the plan view display, after-action review systems, and simulation control systems.

simulation time The simulator's internal representation of Greenwich Mean Time (GMT). Simulation time may accumulate faster than, slower than, or at the same pace as GMT.

simulator (1) A device, computer program, or system that performs simulation. (2) For training, a device that duplicates the essential features of a task situation and provides for direct practice. (3) For DIS, a physical model or simulation of a weapons system, a set of weapons systems, or a piece of equipment that represents some major aspects of the equipment's operation.

Simworld A collection of simulation entity types and simulation asset types that can be used together to create a synthetic environment. See also *Simworld database.*

Simworld database (SWDB) A standard, configuration-managed library of machine-independent information that is structured in the form of types of simulation entities and simulation assets. In practice, simulation entities and simulation assets within a Simworld will meet some defined interoperability criteria. See also *Simworld.*

site (1) An actual physical location at a specific geographic area (e.g., the Fort Knox close combat test bed [CCTB]) that can contain a single cell, multiple cells, or only part of a cell. (2) A node on the DIS long-haul network that can contain a single cell, multiple cells, or only part of a cell. (3) A level of configuration authority within a DIS exercise.

site manager The individual responsible for the maintenance and operation of the simulators and local-area network operations to support the requirements of the users. Additional responsibilities include safety, data collection, and providing appropriate terrain and appropriate information for training feedback, such as after-action reviews and take-home packages. See also *site.*

slow time The duration of activities within a simulation in which simulated time advances slower than actual time. Contrast with *fast time; real time.*

smoothing Interpolation of the last state vector of entity state Protocol Data Units to the current state vector, creating a smoothed transition between two successive state vector updates.

software model A symbolic model whose properties are expressed in software; for example, a computer program that models the effects of climate on the world economy. Contrast with *graphical model; mathematical model; narrative model; tabular model.*

sponsor The organization that obtains the modeling and simulation use rights from the owner, assumes overall responsibility, and pays the user on behalf of the proponent.

stabilized-variable model A model in which some of the variables are held constant and others are allowed to vary; for example, a model of a controlled climate in which humidity is held constant and temperature is allowed to vary.

standard cell A cell that is compliant with the DIS message and database standards.

state (1) The internal status of a simulation entity (e.g., fuel level, number of rounds remaining, location of craters). State messages are used to start and restart entities or to update entities concerning the dynamic changes in the environment in their area of interest. See also *simulation entity.* (2) A condition or mode of existence that a system, component, or simulation may be in; for example, the preflight state of an aircraft navigation program or the input state of a given channel. (3) The values assumed at a given instant by the variables that define the characteristics of a system, component, or simulation. Also called system state. See also *final state; initial state; steady state.*

state machine A model of a system in which all values are discrete, as in a digital computer.

state transition A change from one state to another in a system, component, or simulation.

state variable A variable that defines one of the characteristics of a system, component, or simulation. The values of all such variables define the state of the system, component, or simulation.

static model A model of a system in which there is no change; for example, a scale model of a bridge, studied for its appearance rather than for its performance under varying loads. Contrast with *dynamic model.*

statistics collection Information on network transmission timing and events. Used for transmission management, network monitoring, network and component performance assessments, and tuning.

steady state A situation in which a model, process, or device exhibits stable behavior independent of time. Also called equilibrium.

stimulate To provide input to a system in order to observe or evaluate the system's response.

stimulator (1) A hardware device that injects or radiates signals into the sensor system(s) of operational equipment to imitate the effects of platforms, munitions, and environment that are not physically present. (2) A battlefield entity consisting of hardware and/or software modules that injects signals directly into the sensor systems of an actual battlefield entity to simulate other battlefield entities in the virtual battlefield.

stochastic Pertaining to a process, model, or variable whose outcome, result, or value depends on chance. Contrast with *deterministic.*

stochastic model A model in which the results are determined by using one or more random variables to represent uncertainty about a process or in which a given input will produce an output according to some statistical distribution; for example, a model that estimates the total dollars spent at each of the checkout stations in a supermarket, based on probable number of customers and probable purchase amount of each customer. Also called probabilistic model. See also *Markov chain model.* Contrast with *deterministic model.*

structural model A representation of the physical or logical structure of a system; for example, a representation of a computer network as a set of boxes connected by communication lines. Contrast with *process model.*

symbolic model A model whose properties are expressed in symbols. Examples include graphic models, mathematical models, narrative models, software models, and tabular models. Contrast with *physical model.*

synthetic environment The representation of the real world through simulation (the implementation environment); composed of simulation entities, the simulation environment, and their interactions. Also called electronic battlefield; virtual world.

system state See *state.*

tabular model A symbolic model whose properties are expressed in tabular form; for example, a truth table that represents the logic of an OR gate. Contrast with *graphic model; mathematical model; narrative model; software model.*

TCTS Tactical Combat Training System.

time The measurable aspect of duration. Time makes use of scales based on the occurrence of periodic events. These are the day, depending on the rotation of the earth; the month, depending on the revolution of the moon around the earth; and the year, depending on the revolution of the earth around the sun. Time is expressed as a length on a duration scale measured from an index on that scale. For example: 4 P.M. local mean solar time means that four mean solar hours have elapsed since the mean sun was on the meridian of the observer.

time-dependent event An event that occurs at a predetermined point in time or after a predetermined period of time has elapsed. See also *conditional event.*

time-flow mechanism The approach used locally by an individual federate to perform time advancement. Commonly used time-flow mechanisms include event-driven (or event-stepped), time-driven, and independent time advance (real-time synchronization) mechanisms.

time-interval simulation See *time-slice simulation.*

time management A collection of mechanisms and services to control the advancement of time within each federate during an execution in a way that is consistent with federation requirements for message ordering and delivery.

time-slice simulation (1) A discrete simulation that is terminated after a specific amount of time has elapsed; for example, a model depicting the year-by-year forces affecting a volcanic eruption over a period of 100,000 years. Also called time-interval simulation. See also *critical event simulation.* (2) A discrete simulation of continuous events in which time advances by intervals chosen independent of the simulated events; for example, a model of a time multiplexed communication system with multiple channels transmitting signals over a single transmission line in very rapid succession.

time stamp A value representing a point on the federation time axis that is assigned to an event to indicate when that event is said to occur. Certain message ordering services are based on this time stamp value. In constrained simulations, the time stamp may be viewed as a deadline indicating the latest time at which the message notifying the federate of the event may be processed.

time stamp order (TSO) A total ordering of messages based on the "temporally happens before" ($\rightarrow_t$) relationship. A message delivery service is said to be time stamp ordered if for any two messages M_1 and M_2 (containing notifications of events E_1 and E_2, respectively) that are delivered to a single federate where $E_1 \rightarrow_t E_2$, then M_1 is delivered to the federate before M_2. The Runtime Infrastructure (RTI) ensures that any two TSO messages will be delivered to all federates receiving both messages in the same relative order. To ensure this, the RTI uses a consistent tie-breaking mechanism to ensure that all federates perceive the same ordering of events containing the same time stamp. Further, the tie-breaking mechanism is deterministic, meaning that repeated executions of the federation will yield the same relative ordering of these events if the same initial conditions and inputs are used and all messages are transmitted using time stamp ordering.

time variable A variable whose value represents simulated time or the state of the simulation clock.

tracked munition A munition for which tracking data are required. A tracked munition's flight path is represented by entity state Protocol Data Units (PDUs).

transmit management The control of the transmission rate to match the transmission media. The transmission rate is selected to reduce total network traffic.

transportation service A Runtime Infrastructure–provided service for transmitting messages between federates. Different categories of service are defined with different characteristics regarding reliability of delivery and message ordering.

true global time A federation-standard representation of time synchronized to Greenwich Mean Time or Universal Time Coordinated (as defined in this glossary) with or without some offset (positive or negative) applied.

tutorial simulation See *instructional simulation.*

unbundling The process of unpacking bundled Protocol Data Units (PDUs) into multiple separate PDUs.

unconstrained simulation A simulation in which there is no explicit relationship between wall-clock time and the rate of time advancements. These are sometimes called "as-fast-as-possible" simulations, and these two terms are used synonymously here. Analytical simulation models and many constructive war-game simulations are unconstrained simulations.

unicast A transmission mode in which a single message is sent to a single network destination (i.e., one to one).

unit An aggregate of entities.

unit conversion A system of converting measurement from one basis to another; for example, English/metric, knots/feet per second, IEEE floating point, byte swapping.

Universal Time Coordinated (UTC) The same as Greenwich Mean Time. A nonuniform time based on the rotation of the earth, which is not constant. Usually referred to as, Coordinated Universal Time.

users Military, industrial, or academic organizations requiring access to the DIS network. Prior to use, they appoint one point of responsibility for their use of the network. This person is the exercise manager.

validation The formal process of determining the degree to which a model or simulation is an accurate representation of the real world from the perspective of the intended uses of the model or simulation.

variable A quantity or data item whose value can change. See also *dependent variable; independent variable; state variable.*

verbal-descriptive model See *narrative model.*

verification The formal process of determining that a model implementation accurately represents the developer's conceptual description and specifications; also, the formal process of determining whether a simulation model performs as intended.

verification and validation (V&V) proponent The agency responsible for ensuring that V&V are performed on a specific model or simulation.

virtual battlefield The illusion resulting from simulating the actual battlefield. Also called electronic battlefield.

virtual network The interconnection of DIS cells by any communications means that provides the necessary network services to conduct an exercise.

virtual time See *simulated time.*

virtual world See *synthetic environment.*

visual stealth A component that provides the capabilities for visually observing a DIS exercise without participating in the DIS exercise interaction.

wall-clock time A federate's measurement of true global time, where the measurand is typically output from a hardware clock. The error in this measurement can be expressed as an algebraic residual between wall-clock time and true global time or as an amount of estimation uncertainty associated with the wall-clock time measurement software and the hardware clock errors.

war game A simulation game in which participants seek to achieve a specified military objective, given preestablished resources and constraints; for example, a simulation in which participants make battlefield decisions and a computer determines the results of those decisions. Also called constructive simulation; higher-order model (HOM). See also *management game.*

warfare simulation A model of warfare or any part of warfare for any purpose (such as analysis or training).

WGS–84 World geodetic system 1984.

white box model See *glass box model.*

wide-area network (WAN) A communications network of devices that are separated by substantial geographic distance. Also called long-haul network.

world coordinate system The right-handed geocentric Cartesian system. The shape of the world is described by the WGS 84 standard. The origin of the world coordinate system is the centroid of the earth. The axes of this system are labeled X, Y, and Z, with the positive X-axis passing through the prime meridian at the equator, the positive Y-axis passing through 90 degrees east longitude at the equator and the positive Z-axis passing through the North Pole. See also *WGS 84.*

world view The view that each simulation entity maintains of the simulated world from its own vantage point, based on the results of its own simulation and its processing of event messages received from all external entities. For computer-generated forces, the world view is part of the state of the entity. For manned simulators of real vehicles, the world view is the perceptions of the participating humans.

yoked variable One of two or more variables that are dependent on one another in such a manner that a change in one automatically causes a change in the others.

Index

Advanced Concept Technology Demonstrations, 7
Air Force Institute of Technology, 61
Air Force Modeling and Simulation, 124–25
Air Tasking Order process, 74
Architecture. *See* High Level Architecture
Architecture Management Group, 96, 98
Army Simulation, Training, and Instrumentation Command, 121–22
ARPANET, 29
Arsenal Ship concept, 79–81
ATO. *See* Air Tasking Order process

Battle of 73 Easting, 1, 2, 8
Battlefield Awareness and Data Dissemination, 7
Battlespace, definition of, 54
  dominance, 54
  visualization, 54
Boorda, Jeremy, Admiral, 9
  on virtual simulation technology, 94
Bosnia training simulator, 53–54

Canadian Cup battle, 8
Cartesian coordinate system, 39–40
Clausewitzian principles, 4
CNN phenomenon, 4
Combat identification of friend or foe, 75–76
Combined Arms Tactical Trainer, 49–50
Command and Control simulation facility, 59–60
Compliance testing, 87
Conventional Targeting Effectiveness Model, 74, 105
Coordinate systems, simulation, 39–41
Crisis action concept exploration, 74–75
CTEM. *See* Conventional Targeting Effectiveness Model

Dahmann, Judith, Dr., 11–12, 99
DARPA. *See* Defense Advanced Research Projects Agency
Data dictionary, Department of Defense, 100
DCSOPS. *See* Deputy Chief of Staff for Operations and Plans

Dead Reckoning, 27–29
Defense Advanced Research Projects Agency, 11, 119–20
Defense Modeling and Simulation Tactical Technology Information Analysis Center, 126–27
Defense Modeling and Simulation Initiative, 115–17
Defense Modeling and Simulation Office, 85, 118–19
Defense Simulation Internet, 32–34
  encryption, 35
Department of Defense, data dictionary, 100
Deputy Chief of Staff for Operations and Plans, 54
Desert Storm, 1
Deutch, John, Dr., 6
  on dominant battlefield awareness, 91
Digital Terrain Elevation Data, 121
Director for Defense Research and Engineering, 113–15
DIS. *See* Distributed Interactive Simulation
Distributed Interactive Simulation, 2–3, 35
  accreditation, 84–88
  for actionable command and control, 6–7
  ameliorating warfighting deficiences, 8–10
  application opportunities, 72–81
  application questions, 70, 71
  architectures, 82–84
  autonomous simulation applications, 26
  basic concepts for, 25
  conferences, 127
  costs, 88–89
  credibility, 93
  Dead Reckoning, 27–29
  definition of, 14–16
  directions, 10–13
  distributed computing approach, 26
  essential subjects for understanding, 15–16
  execution of warfare relation, 3–5
  expectations for results of, 93
  for exploring troublesome issues, 92–93
  ground truth vs. perception, 26